The Five Approaches to Acting Series

GETTING TO THE TASK

WRITTEN BY DAVID KAPLAN

HPG

Hansen Publishing Group, LLC
East Brunswick, New Jersey
www.hansenpublishing.com

International Standard Book Number: 978-1-60182-181-2

Hansen Publishing Group, LLC
302 Ryders Lane
East Brunswick, New Jersey
732-220-1211
www.hansenpublishing.com

CREDITS

To Edwin W. Schloss,

Prince of friends, open-hearted, open-eyed.

CONTENTS

SCRIPT ANALYSIS COMPARATIVE REFERENCE CHART

	TASK/ACTION ANALYSIS	EPISODIC ANALYSIS	BUILDING IMAGES ANALYSIS	WORLD OF THE PLAY ANALYSIS	NARRATIVE ANALYSIS
BASIC UNIT	Task	Episode	Image	Social context; behavior and form	Event Point of view
ILLUSION OF CHARACTER	Web of relationships	Playing the opposition	String of masks	Distinctions within the context of the world	Intersection of point of view and events
DRAMATIC ACTION	Action meeting an obstacle	Transaction or *gest*	Moment when mask changes	Breach in the rules of the world	Shifting the point of view
KEY QUESTION	What do I need to do?	What do I do? What is my role?	What is this like? What does this make me think of?	What are the values of the world?	What am I describing? What is my point of view?
UNIFYING IMAGE	Oil painting	Poster	Collage	Frame	Film camera angles
RELATIVE THEORY	Freud Psychoanalysis	Alfred Adler Transactional analysis Marxism	Carl Jung Personae	Ruth Benedict Cultural anthropology	Derrida Literary deconstructionism
SUITABLE PLAYWRIGHTS	Chekhov Ibsen Strindberg	Shakespeare Brecht Ionesco	Strindberg Lorca Genet Williams	Molière Wilde O'Neill Beckett	Shakespeare the Greeks Williams Shepard
AUDIENCE	Compassionate	Judgmental	Passionate	Transported	Participatory

PART I

GETTING TO THE TASK

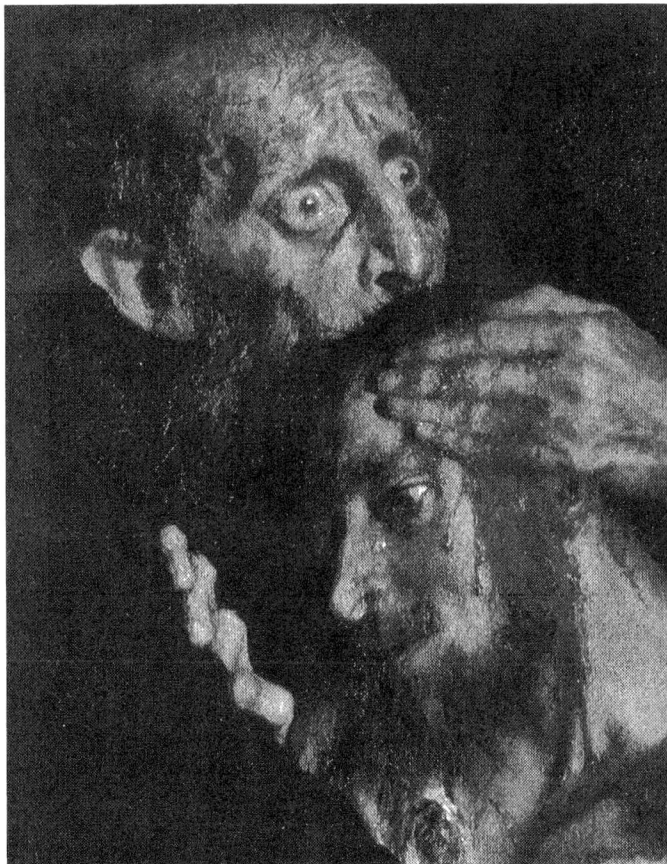

Reading List

The Lesson by Eugene Ionesco
Hedda Gabler by Henrik Ibsen
An Actor Prepares (chapters 3, 5, 7, and 15) by Konstantin Stanislavsky
Stanislavsky in Focus (chapters 3 and 4) by Sharon Marie Carnicke

Viewing List

Orphans of the Storm directed by D.W. Griffith
A Place in the Sun directed by George Stevens

Ilya Repin, detail from *Ivan the Terrible and His Son Ivan: 16 November 1581*

CHAPTER 1

WHAT SHOULD I DO?

Why Is Stanislavsky Important?

Russia is cold and theaters are warm. For this reason, among other reasons, attending the theater in Russia is and was extraordinarily popular. One hundred years before the American Revolution, demand for theater was so strong in Russia that foreign companies and stars braved the distance, the cold, and the lack of dependably hot water to perform there. Inspired by their visitors to form acting companies of their own, Russian actors learned to imitate the popular European styles of exaggerated poses and singsong declamation. By the end of the nineteenth century—twenty years before the start of the Russian Revolution—Russian actors too were tearing their hair to show despair, placing their hands over their hearts to indicate love, and—reliable report has it—staring open-mouthed with wonder at the mention of death.

A prematurely gray young man from a wealthy family in Moscow (they manufactured gold thread) (1) changed all that, not only in Russia, but in theaters throughout the world. He was stagestruck at the age of three, when he set the tree branch in his hands on fire while playing the role of "Winter" (2). On a business trip to Paris he enrolled in the famous Conservatory and began to study the craft of performing. To save his family embarrassment, he exchanged his last name (Alexeyev) for that of a Polish actor who was retiring from the stage. From then on he was known as Konstantin Stanislavsky. He is the Orville Wright of actors: he taught us to fly. Stanislavsky's soaring approach to acting had no use for hand-over-the-heart sincerity or the pregnant pause. His concern was the spiritual life of an actor, as a creative as well as interpretive artist.

Find the bag of nails

Stanislavsky always claimed he gained his practical insights by watching the performances of two Italian actors, Eleonora Duse and Tommaso Salvini. Although they never acted together, Duse and Salvini both shaped their art with passion and precision; it was this mix that prompted Stanislavsky to develop the craft of creative acting.

Many people had seen Duse and Salvini perform without understanding how these artists accomplished their effects. Most critics discussed what Salvini and Duse did by describing what they did not do. Salvini, though he acted in the grand manner of vivid gestures and thrilling speech, seemed to live on the stage—as if nothing offstage entered his mind. Duse acted in a subtler way; it seemed as if she came from no school at all. She made no displays of any kind, no effort to impress; she didn't make her voice sound interesting, she didn't even wear make-up. Yet out of this seeming nothingness, these two actors took the stages of the world by storm.

It was Stanislavsky who understood the technique of the great Italians. The best example of Stanislavsky's insight is from *An Actor Prepares*, the title given by his American translator to the first of three influential books on training actors. By his fifth page, Stanislavsky is describing a student, whose invented surname, Nazvanov, means "The Chosen One" in Russian (3). Nazvanov, though doing nothing more than sitting on the stage, is unable to rehearse—much less act. He feels oppressed by the size of the stage floor and pulled into the black hole of the audience. Then a workman drops a bag of nails that scatter along the floor. The Chosen One gets on his hands and knees to find the nails, and—for the first time—he feels at home on the stage. Stanislavsky expands on this later when a group of students hunt for a lost pin and a lost purse. Why did searching look and feel real, while simply sitting onstage looked and felt fake? Because individually or as a group, when actors are looking for something, they have *a task*.

That's the first step toward all else that follows: A TASK.

The essence of Stanislavsky's thinking is that behavior and emotions are functions of *wanting to do something for a purpose* on the stage. Behavior and emotion derive from desire. In the illustrations above, the students want to pick up nails or find a pin. That's their purpose for being onstage, rather than to make a display of themselves to the audience. In this way, their simple hunt parallels the sophisticated acting of Duse and Salvini; their emotions are convincing because they derive from *purpose*. When they find a nail, they're happy. When a nail rolls away from them, they're frustrated, but continue in their pursuit.

This was Stanislavsky's radical idea—radical in the real meaning of the word, because it uprooted the rules of acting. Instead of defining behavior, it defined *motivation* as the technical basis of good acting. This was not an original idea of Stanislavsky's, but his genius was to include the art of acting in a trend that was developing in Western culture at the same time.

Inner drama in fiction

A comparable transition had begun at least fifty years before, in another art form with conventions for characters and plot: the novel. In nineteenth-century Europe and America, novels occupied the place in mass culture that film occupies today. For those who could read and the many more who liked to be read to, novels provided—at a comfortably safe distance—visits to exotic places and the vicarious experience of other people's lives. We get an idea of the novel's popular appeal when we read that anxious crowds lined the docks of New York in 1841 to secure the latest serial installment of Charles Dickens's novel *The Old Curiosity Shop*—just to learn what had happened to its pathetic heroine, Little Nell. They weren't asking about the snappy dialogue or secret motives. They wanted to know what happened.

Since the days of Robinson Crusoe racing from the cannibals, what authors offered their audiences were narratives composed of curious events succeeded by events curiouser and curiouser. This happened, that happened, and any and all of what happened next was external and describable. As its title suggests, *The Old Curiosity Shop* has much to offer in the "what happened" department, and a cast of colorful characters to whom these things happen. There is an ugly yet strangely attractive dwarf, with the memorable name of Quilp, who steals the life savings from a good but gullible man. There is the gullible good man's noble granddaughter, frail Little Nell, who lies languishing near death for a few suspenseful chapters. "Is Little Nell dead?" the crowds shouted as the boat with the latest installment docked into New York harbor. *What had happened?*

Other writers, though, many of them women, were interested in *why* events and behavior happened.* In England, thirty years before Little Nell, Jane Austen wrote novels in which the unspoken machinations of matchmaking were laid bare. Even her titles—*Sense and Sensibility, Pride and Prejudice*—demonstrate a clash of ideas, not arms. Austen knew herself enough to politely decline an invitation from the Court of Queen Victoria to write a historical adventure in the style of the sword-and-maiden specialist Walter Scott. Scott himself understood the difference between his and Austen's styles, and referred to his own work, books like *Ivanhoe*, as written in the "bow-wow style."

By the middle of the century, George Eliot, an Englishwoman with the mask of a masculine name, used her powerful intelligence to create novels that portrayed the *inner drama* of characters. Her first novel was called *Adam Bede* (1859), and there was adventure enough in it: Adam Bede is a modest carpenter in love with a poor woman who appears to have killed her own child. Significantly, the novel continues for an eighth of its length after the woman's execution and describes what could never be seen in an adventure, or written in a letter, or even thought about consciously: how Adam is restored to life by wrestling with his anguish, "which he must think of as renewed with the light of every new morning" (4). George Eliot made the processes of wrestling with feelings seem as dramatic and interesting as adventures. Her books included the evolution of characters—not only what happened to them, but also the adventure of what happened *inside them.*

Other novelists in other places unveiled the drama of inner action, sometimes enhancing it by contrasting it with outer action. In France, Gustave Flaubert's novel *Madame Bovary* (1857) presented the romantic drama of a bored middle-class woman who imagines that she has found true love outside her marriage with an adventurer. Flaubert ironically stirred his heroine's sentimental dreams into the muck of her real-life entanglement. Emma Bovary eventually kills herself when her adventurer leaves her. About the same time as Flaubert, over in America, Herman Melville was writing

---

*Since the Renaissance, there were novels—in Spain, in France, in England—made up of collections of imaginary letters that gave insight into the diverse thoughts and points of view of different characters, even as they described adventures.

Moby Dick—a meditation on a whale hunt, rather than the series of sea adventures that his previous two novels had been. In 1881, the American émigré Henry James wrote *Washington Square*, in which very little of what we would call adventure takes place. The novel's principle action is that a young heiress does *not* get married.

James admired Eliot's quiet insight and Flaubert's irony, and though indifferent to the example of his countryman Melville, he was especially impressed by the person and the writings of a Russian novelist who lived in Paris, Ivan Turgenev. Turgenev's novels delicately and subtly depicted characters whose drama was their lack of drama (James particularly liked that nothing happened). Turgenev's heroes were incapable of heroism; his heroines *didn't* consummate their love affairs. Another Russian master of internal action was Leo Tolstoy, who began his writing career with the intention of becoming an adventure writer—the Russian Walter Scott—but ended up punctuating his battle scenes in novels like *War and Peace* with his characters' equally momentous internal battles.

It might be said that the Russian emphasis on internal drama in fiction culminated in the work of Fyodor Dostoyevsky, whose writing traces the beautiful ambiguity of motivation. In his *Crime and Punishment* (1866), the main character takes nine pages to kill an old lady—and over four hundred pages to agonize about it before he confesses (in two pages). The condemned killer's train ride to exile in Siberia—which must have been a long and agonizing experience—is mentioned in an aside. Dostoyevsky demonstrates that what goes on in a person's mind can be forty-five times more dramatic than what that person does or says, even if—and maybe *especially* if—that person is an ax murderer.

Dostoyevsky's reputation grew in the 1880s, about the same time Stanislavsky began his search for substance in the art of acting. It was Stanislavsky's ambition to put onstage, and make dramatic, the inner process of the actor—to reach to the substance that Dostoyevsky was mining when he detailed the inner processes of the characters in his novels. Stanislavsky's interest in revealing the inner process of acting was not just technical, or even aesthetic. His commitment was based on compassion, and he rode the wave of a social movement—at that point unnamed—that sympathized with all people of all classes. George Eliot was part of that movement too, as she wrote in *Adam Bede*:

> These fellow mortals, every one, must be accepted as they are: you can neither straighten their noses, nor brighten their wit, nor rectify their dispositions; and it is these people—amongst whom your life is passed—that it is needful you should tolerate, pity, love: it is these more or less ugly, stupid, inconsistent people whose movements of goodness you should be able to admire—for whom you should cherish all possible hopes, all possible patience. And I would not, even if I had the choice, be the clever novelist who could create a world so much better than this, in which we get up in the morning to do our daily work, that you would be likely to turn a harder, colder eye on the dusty streets and the common green fields—on the real breathing men and women, who can be chilled by your indifference or injured by your prejudice; who can be cheered and helped onward by your fellow-feeling, your forbearance, your outspoken brave justice.

So I am content to tell my simple story without trying to make things seem better than they were; dreading nothing, indeed, but falsity, which in spite of one's best efforts, there is reason to dread. Falsehood is so easy, truth so difficult. The pencil is conscious of a delightful facility in drawing a griffin—the longer the claws, and the larger the wings, the better; but that marvelous facility which we mistook for genius is apt to forsake us when we want to draw a real unexaggerated lion. Examine your words well, and you will find that even when you have no motive to be false, it is a very hard thing to say the exact truth, even about your own immediate feelings—much harder than to say something fine about them which is *not* the exact truth (5).

Inner drama in art

Stanislavsky was a cultured man—his first important job was to chair a *Society of Art and Literature*, which was, in part, an amateur theater where he directed. His search for ways to depict the truth, while stimulated by the achievement of Russian writers, was also shaped by the assumptions of Russian painters. In the visual arts, as in theater, Russia had copied Western Europe by setting up a state Academy that taught artists to draw from plaster casts of Greek statues and to paint with a technique that blended oil paints to a porcelain finish. Art students were assigned subjects from classical mythology or the Bible.

In France, artists rebelled against Academy training by painting subjects from life, not plaster casts. They applied paint so that it blended in the eye of the viewer, not on the canvas. The *Impressionists* painted subject matter significant for its physical beauty, whatever its cultural associations, negative or positive, traditional or contemporary. If there happened to be social implications to French subject matter, and there could be (squalid drunks or stolid bourgeoisie), those social concerns were secondary to the new ways of seeing form and new methods of applying paint.

Russian painters rebelled against their Academy in a different way. Their technique of applying paint stayed roughly the same, but their subject matter changed dramatically. *Genre painting* depicting scenes of recognizable middle-class life (which, by the way, George Eliot claimed to be her inspiration) was already a convention throughout Europe, but Russian painters, moved by the miserable circumstances of their country, made genre painting pointedly political and topical. The *Itinerants*—so called by themselves because they had no fixed place to show their work or, at times, to live—painted contemporary and often dramatic events: fathers unexpectedly coming home from prison, a woman bravely handing out pamphlets to poor people, a bank failure, smug policemen guarding a religious procession. French Impressionist artists most often painted a model's vague cheerfulness or detached and moody pensiveness, a sort of rainy-day patience that was probably an honest representation of the model's mood while posing. Russian Itinerant painters *staged scenes*, like theater directors.

Look, for example, at Nikolai Yaroshenko's *Life Is Everywhere*, painted in 1888. It requires an explanation today, but its meaning was clear to the public when it was first painted. It is a picture of a scuffed boxcar, and resembles a still frame from a filmstrip.

The initials on the side of the boxcar indicate that it is transporting prisoners to Siberia. Inside the car, a woman holds a grinning baby up to the bars of a window. The child reaches out through the bars. He's throwing crumbs to pigeons that have gathered below the window. A smiling man inside the boxcar holds a chunk of brown bread in his weathered hand, which just touches the child's pink fingers. Behind them is an older man with a beard, and another middle-aged man's face topped by a cap. They crowd behind the mother so that they may share the baby's pleasure. Another figure in the boxcar, seen from the back, stares out at the blank sky through the bars of the opposite window. With its blended color and even lighting, the style of the painting is not that different from academic technique. Yet Yaroshenko utilized that technique to evoke the child's pleasure—and doing so he portrayed the ironic *relationship* between the caged prisoners forcibly carted to Siberia and the birds free to fly away south.

The Russians were certainly not the first to paint relationships or contemporary political events, but the Itinerants were seized with a mission to make psychological subject matter worthy of investigation and refinement in its own right. Even episodes taken from the Bible or Russian history were illustrated for psychological and social significance. A wonderful example is a small canvas painted by Ilya Repin entitled *Ivan the Terrible and His Son Ivan: 16 November 1581*. Actually, the Russian word is not "Terrible," it is *Grozny*, and this painting helps to explain the meaning of the word. *Grozny* means more than terrible; it is related to the Russian word for thunderstorm, *groza*. *Grozny* implies fear and wonder and the breath-catching response to an overwhelming storm. There is something of this in the root meaning of the English word *awful*—"full of awe."

On November 16, 1581, Tsar Ivan *Grozny* quarreled with his son and killed him with a fire poker. Repin depicts this event in the painting as if it were on stage. The evidence of the murder is literally in front of the viewer: the bloody fire poker lies in the foreground three inches from the edge of the frame. The bottom half of the painting is a red Oriental rug, rumpled as it would be after a struggle. Repin painted this work in 1885, and its subject matter—the Tsar killing the younger generation—resonated with its viewers. This was a period in Russian history analogous to 1960s America for its liberalism and the reaction liberalism provoked. Parricide was the subject of Dostoyevsky's *The Brothers Karamazov* of 1880 and Turgenev's *Fathers and Sons* a few years before that. The meaning of the painting was not lost on the then-reigning Tsar. On his personal order, the canvas was removed from its gallery.

But this painting is significant even beyond its politics. At the same time in France, Seurat was dabbing on points of color to portray *Sunday Afternoon on the Island of La Grand Jatte*, and Monet was whisking feathery brushstrokes onto canvas to depict the changes of light on the façade of the Rouen Cathedral. Yet nothing in the well-known French Impressionist art of the 1880s prepares a viewer for the psychological depth Russian Itinerant painters achieved. What artists in the West dismiss to this day as sentimental genre painting, nineteenth-century Russian artists developed into a high art.

The greatness of Repin's painting is not in its technical innovations. This is a great painting because the artist—using crushed rocks mixed with oil pressed from seeds, applied with an animal's hair tied to a stick, and spread onto dried grass—has given form to an unspeakable but universal feeling: the horror of a sin that cannot be atoned for. *Grozny*. Awe-ful. In Repin's scene the Tsar cradles his dying son's head. The open eye of the son indicates that he is still alive. He knows that he is dying and he stares at his own blood with wonder and surprise. The father looks out, his eyes focused on what seems to be a vast depth. The surroundings, the furniture, the lighting, the gestures, the facial expressions—all are meant to involve the viewer in a psychological relationship with the subject matter, to evoke compassion for the murdered and for the murderer.

Just as Repin used the physical materials of paint to express the immaterial, it was Stanislavsky's ambition to create a craft for actors that could rouse the spiritual power of their art. His search for a way to tap into the power of the mind drew from various sources in art and literature—as well as Indian Yogic teachings that the mind and body were indivisible. The mechanism Stanislavsky eventually conceived was his own, yet it closely paralleled groundbreaking psychological theories that were being developed at the same time by Sigmund Freud in Vienna.

The science of inner process

Freud's central idea, which marks the beginning of twentieth-century psychology, is that emotions and behavior are functions of desire. People don't do things because a genie slips into their ear during the night. People don't have bad dreams because they eat spoiled fruit before bed. People do things, including dream, because they have desires. These may not be conscious desires, but conscious or not, desires structure behavior.

One of Freud's essential contributions to an understanding of desire and human relationships is this: what you want but never get means more in life than what you want and *do* get. Beginning with desire for a parent, which Freud called the *Electra* and *Oedipus complexes*, some desires inevitably meet immovable obstacles. In the case of lust for a parent, social convention and incest taboos are such obstacles.

The names Electra and Oedipus are taken from Greek plays where characters with these names meet tragic ends when their desires are revealed or perversely fulfilled. But in life, thwarted desires don't usually meet tragic ends. Once desires meet an obstacle, they don't die; they retreat into the mind, below the surface of awareness, in the region called the *subconscious*. According to Freud, because gratified desires have been relieved and their energy spent, character is determined more by thwarted desires that remain in the subconscious to linger or fester unsatisfied—and unseen.

Thwarted desires determine character more than gratified desires. We'll soon see how this theory parallels Stanislavsky's work. According to Freud (and Stanislavsky), in order to understand and *choose* appropriate behavior with which to encounter obstacles in the world, one needs to move beyond conscious explanations and reach down to the subconscious. There one can view and identify unseen desire.

Neither Freud nor Stanislavsky ever heard of the other, although the foundations of Freud's research began in 1888, almost simultaneously with Stanislavsky's research into a performer's use of the subconscious.*

Stanislavsky's investigation below the conscious mind for the source of behavior was sustained not by psychology, but by his life-long interest in Yoga. The Indian religious approach called Yoga has many paths. Stanislavsky was interested in two of them: *Hatha Yoga* and *Raja Yoga*. Hatha Yoga, the more familiar, teaches the mind to observe the processes of the body in order to relax and ultimately eradicate stress. Raja Yoga, more pertinent here, teaches the mind to observe its inner desires in order to choose which desires to pursue, but only to refine and ultimately *eradicate* desire. Stanislavsky, however, differs from Raja Yoga when he asks that the actor's mind observe its inner desires in order to creatively *pursue* desire.

Terms to Work with: Tasks and Actions

This chapter limits itself to the ways Stanislavsky suggested that an actor organize a text with a structure of motivation. Even that is complex. Drawing ideas from several sources, Stanislavsky developed his insights during forty years of rehearsals, performances, and classes, eventually organizing them into a system for working in the theater. Today, around the world, the study of the *Stanislavsky System* is a field of its own. In theory or in practice, it takes more than a lifetime to master it. Stanislavsky wrote about this system expansively. The vast majority of his writing was taken down as notes and notebooks for himself, and never intended for publication. Some writings were published during his lifetime; most were not. When Stanislavsky died, a state commission was formed to sort through and organize the thousands of pages in manuscript he left behind. Nine volumes of the *Collected Stanislavsky* have been published in Russia, several of them multiple books—and some very different from their English "translations."

Stanislavsky's theories on acting have not only been translated into the many languages of the world, they've been translated into the many fancies of various acting teachers. Each teacher seems to have his own vocabulary of words that express the same basic ideas. The written word is just as suspect: at the turn of the twenty-first century, the field has cracked open once again with evidence—brought forward by American scholar Sharon Marie Carnicke—that the American translation of the most influential of Stanislavsky's books is abridged and inaccurate, and that the Soviet version of the same book is censored. More than a hundred years after the start of the Russian Revolution in acting, the full breadth of Stanislavsky's contribution has yet to be published, much less read, understood, or applied.

Many ideas about Stanislavsky in America were passed down orally from teacher to

---

*The psychologist whom Stanislavsky did read was the Frenchman Théodule Ribot, who claimed that a very small number of the sixty people he surveyed on the subject were so affected by emotional experience that the memory of past sensations was ingrained in their bodies. When so-called "affective memories" were recalled, they supposedly revived both sensation and emotion. Stanislavsky used Ribot's theory as support for his own investigations into memory and emotion, deciding on his own that affective memory wasn't rare, but inherent in all people and capable of development in all actors. Even so, Ribot's theory offered no support for an investigation of motivations for action.

student and repeated. One of the reasons for the variations in American interpretations is the American mishearing of Russian accents in English. During the very first speech about Stanislavsky's system in America, listeners took notes as the speaker mentioned the importance of *"beets"*—segments of a scene determined by a single task. Did the speaker mean "beats" as in musical "beats" (as some thought)? Was it "bits" as in show-biz "bits" (as someone claimed to have heard from Stanislavsky himself)? Was it "beads" on a string? Or was it Borscht?*

What's called the "Stanislavsky System" and how close it is to what Stanislavsky actually said, wrote, or meant, you can spend your life arguing. Don't. For the purposes of this text, these are the terms that an actor faced with a script can use. Learn them and you can put them to use in your work.

Task

The basic premise of Stanislavsky's approach to acting is that the text sets a **task**, which in turn challenges an actor to answer the question *What do I need to do?* The word we're calling a *task* can also be translated as a *problem*, for which the actor must find a solution. The task provides the need that drives an actor's activities, speeches, relationships, and behavior on stage. Four examples:

- I need to pass this class.
- I need to teach this student a lesson.
- I need to escape this prison of a marriage.
- I need to get back with my old boyfriend.

Within the rules of this approach, the place where a performer tries to satisfy any needs is onstage, and only onstage. You don't try to satisfy your needs out in the audience; an invisible wall stands in your way. Because of the three-sided box-like sets of Stanislavsky's time, this invisible wall became known as *the fourth wall*, closing off the actors from the audience. Because of the fourth wall, although you might need to escape, you don't run off the stage, down the aisles, and out the doors of the theater.

Action

An **action** is what you perform onstage to accomplish the task. The action answers the question *What do I do to get what I need?* An action is written in the form of an *infinitive verb*, in the *active* voice, in the *transitive* case. An action is a verb because it's something that you *do*:

- teach (*not* a teacher)
- study (*not* a student)
- escape (*not* an escapee)

---

*At Le Siècle Stanislavsky Conference in Paris, translators did translate the word as *beets*. Is this the root of organic acting?

The *infinitive* is the simplest form of the verb, always preceded by the word *to*:

- to teach
- to study
- to escape

Actions use verbs in the *active* voice—not the passive voice—because they are something that you do, not something done to you:

- to study (*not* to be taught)
- to escape (*not* to be untied)
- to arouse or to entice (*not* to be desired or to be chased after)

The action is never a state of being. You don't want "to be" anything; you want to do something. You don't want to be passive onstage. Even when you are listening, you want to be listening *actively*:

- I want to enjoy (*not* I want to be happy)
- I want to remove myself (*not* I want to be left alone)
- I want to graduate (*not* I want to be a graduate)

Now for the essential part: The action is expressed as a *transitive* verb because a transitive verb requires an *object* to complete its action. You want to put yourself in an *active relationship* with *somebody else*. For example, if the task is *I need to escape this prison of an acting class*, the actions can be:

- to charm my teacher
- to evade my teacher
- to confuse my teacher
- to beg for mercy from my teacher

The task is not simply *to run* from acting class, but *to escape it*. You want to run? Go ahead. Run! You don't need anyone else to run. But *I want to escape* . . . puts you in a *relationship* with something or someone else. When you are looking for ways to meet your task, you look to the other actors onstage. You may not want to, but that's what's there to look at. In this approach, acting is not the art of emotional display or contented being. Acting is the art of human relationships.

Script analysis

Armed with this information, let's poke at a script. By doing so we are reversing the usual order for working in rehearsal. *Script analysis* is not meant to be something you do at home and then display in the rehearsal hall to the wonder of your colleagues. It's meant to organize your work in rehearsal, and, ideally, it should follow the rehearsal as a way of recording what happened so that you can repeat the circumstances that achieved results.

When he first tried to apply his ideas to rehearsals, Stanislavsky spent a lot of time sitting at a table with his actors analyzing the text for tasks and actions. Later, following the example of Hatha Yoga and its physical exercises meant to unite body and mind (the word *yoga* means *union*), Stanislavsky led his actors to work on their feet at once, so, as he put it, there would be no divide between the spiritual and physical aspects of work. Either way of working is useful for discovering tasks; the way you choose will depend on the play, of course. Some texts are so dense or have so many characters that nothing more than a traffic jam will happen if the early rehearsals begin with the actors standing.

Let's pretend that you've had a rehearsal where you sat at a table and read lines with another actor. The text you read was simple and—seemingly—simple-minded:

> YOUR PART One and one make two, one and two make three, one and three make four, one and four make five.

These are hardly deathless words. You can probably even memorize them without too much trouble. There isn't much leeway in the interpretation of their meaning. They mean what they say. So how would you make them active?

A Web of Relationships: Rehearsing a Scene from *The Lesson*

The lines quoted above are from a scene in Eugene Ionesco's 1954 play, *The Lesson* (6). A Professor who gives lessons at home begins working with a new Pupil. When the Pupil arrives, she is self-assured and intimidates the Professor. The Professor begins the lesson by asking the Pupil a series of comically easy questions. Her quick responses fluster him. Then the Professor's questions get harder. Slowly the balance of power changes. The Professor deliberately confuses the Pupil. He sadistically insists that she answer his trick questions, even when she cries out that she suffers from a painful toothache. Eventually he teaches her how to escape the pain he causes her. He stabs her while teaching her to say the words, "The knife kills."

> PROFESSOR How much are one and one?
>> [The Professor's task is *to trap the Pupil*]
>
> PUPIL One and one make two.
>> [The Pupil's task is *to satisfy the Professor*]
>
> PROFESSOR (*marveling at the* PUPIL'S *knowledge*) Oh, but that's very good. You appear to me to be well along in your studies. You should easily achieve the total doctorate, miss.
>> [The Professor's action is *to flatter the Pupil*]
>
> PUPIL I'm so glad. Especially to have someone like you tell me this.
>> [The Pupil's action is *to soften up the Professor*]

These choices for tasks and actions are by no means the only choices. The lines could be interpreted differently:

> PROFESSOR How much are one and one?
> [task: *to encourage the Pupil*]
>
> PUPIL One and one make two.
> [task: *to earn her degree quickly*]
>
> PROFESSOR (*marveling at the* PUPIL'S *knowledge*) Oh, but that's very good. You appear to me to be well along in your studies. You should easily achieve the total doctorate, miss.
> [action: *to coax the Pupil*]
>
> PUPIL I'm so glad. Especially to have someone like you tell me this.
> [action: *to prod the Professor*]

Either way, the structure of the lines remains the same. The Professor speaks because he wants to fulfil his task. So does the Pupil. The Professor wants to trap the Pupil, so he flatters her. Or he wants to encourage the Pupil, so he coaxes her. The Pupil wants to satisfy the Professor, so she tries to soften him up. Or she wants to get out in a hurry, so she prods him.

Let's accept one set of choices and organize the scene. Although we're exaggerating the change in actions by introducing a new one with practically every sentence, an action can be played for much longer than a line. On the other hand, there can be more than one action to a line. While you're preparing a role, you'll usually use smaller units at first. Later, in rehearsal and performance, the actions will be absorbed into larger ones meant to meet the needs of a task. This resembles learning a dance or gymnastics routine. First you learn the individual steps and repeat them until they flow into each other. Then you can waltz or roll into a somersault without being aware of separate movements (7). What follows is one of many possible interpretations.

> PROFESSOR Let's push on: how much are two and one?
> [task: *to push the Pupil*]
>
> PUPIL Three.
> [task: *to stand up to the Professor*]
>
> PROFESSOR Three and one?
> [action: *to press*]
>
> PUPIL Four.
> [action: *to volley*]
>
> PROFESSOR Four and one?
> [action: *to corner*]
>
> PUPIL Five.
> [action: *to escape*]

PROFESSOR Five and one?
  [action: *to attack*]

PUPIL Six.
  [action: *to protect herself*]

PROFESSOR Six and one?
  [action: *to decoy*]

PUPIL Seven.
  [action: *to snap at*]

PROFESSOR Seven and one?
  [action: *to pounce*]

PUPIL Eight.
  [action: *to satisfy*]

PROFESSOR Seven and one?
  [action: *to trick*]

PUPIL Eight again.
  [action: *to show off*]

PROFESSOR Very well answered. Seven and one?
  [action: *to trick*]

PUPIL Eight once more.
  [action: *to show off*]

PROFESSOR Perfect. Excellent. Seven and one?
  [action: *to set her up, to confuse*]

PUPIL Eight again . . .
  [action: *to bite*]

PUPIL And sometimes nine.
  [action: *to shut him up*]

Activity

The stage direction reads: *marveling at the* PUPIL'S *knowledge*. But *marveling* is not an action, it's an *activity*. Marveling, teaching, questioning, studying, testing, or answering are all activities. The **activity** is the behavior taking place on stage. Bowling, fishing, reading, or looking at a picture album are all activities. The specific activity is determined by the *given circumstances* of the scene, in this case a classroom where studying, testing, and answering are typical activities.

The activity can change and the actions will still be what organize the performance. You may be bowling when you meet your old boyfriend, or you may be showing him a picture album from your honeymoon, but ten-pins or snapshots of tourist traps notwithstanding, your task will still be *to see if your old boyfriend still loves you*. The actions are what you'll do onstage in order to find out if he does.

In the scene from *The Lesson*, the activity, *marveling*, is given by the playwright, but why is the Professor marveling at the Pupil's ability to add one and two? There are many possible choices of actions that would motivate his *marveling*:

- to set the Pupil up
- to get the Pupil to let her guard down
- to seduce the Pupil
- to mock the Pupil

Paradoxically, the activity can be motionless, as when you work on a task with inner actions—*I need to resolve my doubt about my old boyfriend*. At an early period of developing his system, Stanislavsky, mindful of Yoga and concentrating on his own search for inner dramatic action, considered these inner activities far more important artistically than gestures or outer behavior.

Obstacles

The things that stand in your character's way are called **obstacles**. In order to create dramatic action you want to make an obstacle of the other actors. Often they will make obstacles of themselves. You can also make an obstacle out of the physical environment, your costume, or any other aspect of the production or the role. The Professor wants to trip up the Pupil—to dominate her—but she knows the answer to his question. That is the Professor's obstacle.

> PROFESSOR Now, let's look at subtraction. Tell me, if you're not exhausted,
>   how many are four minus three?
>   [His action: *to push her*
>   The obstacle in his way: *she bluffs him*]
> PUPIL Four minus three? . . . Four minus three?
>   [Her action: *to evade him*
>   The obstacle in her way: *he pursues her*]

Opportunities

Although Stanislavsky doesn't mention it directly, you can also identify **opportunities**, those things that will help you to accomplish the task.

> PROFESSOR Yes. I mean to say: subtract three from four.
>   [His task: *to demoralize her*
>   His action: *to corner her*
>   The opportunity: *she is confused and disoriented*]
> PUPIL That makes . . . seven?
>   [Her task: *to save face*

Her action: *to guess the answer*

The opportunity: *the possibility that she might guess correctly*]

PROFESSOR I am sorry but I'm obliged to contradict you. Four minus three does not make seven. You are confused: four plus three makes seven, four minus three does not make seven . . . This is not addition anymore, we must subtract now.

[His task now is *to sabotage the Pupil*

His actions are *to pounce and to punish*

The opportunity is *she gave a wrong answer*]

What Stanislavsky tried to create onstage was an active *web of relationships* among people. To create that active web, the actions you take on stage to accomplish your tasks must be transitive actions that relate to the other actors on the stage. The other actors present obstacles to getting the tasks done, or provide you with opportunities to succeed at your tasks. If you take advantage of the opportunities, or succeed in overcoming the obstacles, your desire is satisfied. If you don't overcome the obstacles, your desire is thwarted. In either case, the outcome is truthful emotion.

- *Completed desire*: I want something from my new professor. I got it. My task is accomplished and I'm happy.
- *Thwarted desire*: I want something from my new professor. I didn't get it. As a result, I am frustrated and angry. I might cry or I might do something desperate.

Don't go onstage and *be* angry, or *be* frustrated. Frustration or anger will come about when you try to meet the demands of your task.

Through-line

Dramatic action, as well as emotion, occur when a task meets up with an obstacle and the actor changes course in the same way that a riverboat pilot on the Mississippi might change course when he finds his craft heading toward an unexpected sandbar. The Russian word for *through-line* is the same word as *channel*, and Stanislavsky makes a point that a pilot navigates his boat down the river by *sticking to the channel*. The diagram Stanislavsky gives for a through-line:

Action ⟶ Obstacle   New Action ⟶ Task

⟍   ⟋

New Action ⟶ Obstacle

The riverboat pilot wants to get from St. Louis to Natchez. But the course of the journey will be altered by any number of circumstances: where the rocks are, where the rapids are, where the banks of the river have shifted. That's the metaphor for organizing the elements of this approach. As you attempt to accomplish your tasks in rehearsal, you will establish a **through-line** by the intersection of action and obstacles. In rehearsal, you want first to identify your tasks and then to establish what helps and what hinders any actions you take to achieve those tasks.

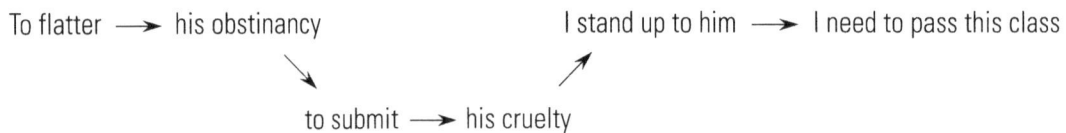

To flatter ⟶ his obstinancy   I stand up to him ⟶ I need to pass this class

    to submit ⟶ his cruelty

Transitions and adjustments

When the Professor redirects himself to his task by trying another action, that tacking movement from *flattering the Pupil* to *coaxing the Pupil* is called **making an adjustment**. The actor makes an adjustment so that he can try a different action in order to meet the demands of the same task. Making adjustments to onstage obstacles is a constant process in rehearsal and in performance. It is what keeps a performance fresh and alive.

When the Professor *accomplishes* his task and moves on to try another task, that switch from *encouraging the Pupil* to *demoralizing the Pupil* is called **making a transition**. The Pupil has been encouraged enough for the Professor to move on and sabotage her. If the Pupil fails at her task and attempts another, that switch also is called making a transition. When she realizes there is no pleasing the Professor, the Pupil might switch to pleading with him. In making the transition, she abandons one task in the face of an immovable obstacle and moves on to a new task that might have more success.

Transitions happen when you switch tasks. That doesn't happen as often as switching actions, but when it does happen, it is more significant. The part of a scene dominated by a single task is experienced by the audience—usually without their being aware of it—as a single unit called a *beat*. Or a bead. Or a bit. You choose.

Super-task

Sometimes a task will challenge a character for the entire play. *I want to teach this girl a lesson*, thinks the Professor. *I want to satisfy my teacher*, thinks the Pupil. This is given the awkward term of **super-task** (it doesn't sound any better in Russian). Harold Clurman, one of the first American stage directors to apply the Stanislavsky System in rehearsals, called the super-task the *spine* of the character. The image is a good one: the spine holds upright and supports.

The advantage of identifying the super-task, or the spine, is that it organizes all the other tasks. You're not just sailing down the river; oh no, you're sailing to Natchez. Practically speaking, when you don't know what to do in performance and rehearsal— or when an unforeseen circumstance happens—you can always fall back on the spine of the character, or hope that the super-task will swoop down from your thoughts and save you from disaster. In Ionesco's *The Lesson*, the Professor's super-task is *to murder the Pupil* or *to teach her a real lesson about life* or *to excite her to rapture* or—any interpretation you choose.

Let's Review Terms

task	what you need to do onstage
action	what you do to accomplish your task
activity	your behavior while you're acting on your task
obstacle	whatever interrupts the progress of your actions
opportunity	what helps you get the task done
super-task	what you need to do throughout the play
making a transition	moving from task to task
making an adjustment	moving from action to action when you encounter an obstacle
through-line	a repeatable progression of actions encountering obstacles and opportunities

The Chart

At the beginning of the book is a chart that compares five different ways of organizing and analyzing a text. There are categories for each form, including *basic unit, dramatic action, key question,* and *relative theory.*

- **Basic unit.** The basic unit is the building block of each system; the way the actor will organize the text. For Stanislavsky, a dramatic text is analyzed and organized into basic units of *tasks.*
- **Dramatic action.** For the actor, dramatic action is what is meant to happen onstage when the words of the play are spoken aloud and performed. In this technique, an *action meant to accomplish a task should meet an obstacle.*
- **Key question.** Like a key unlocking a door to understanding, the basic unit often answers a question. For Stanislavsky the key question is *What do I need to do?*
- **Relative theory.** Acting is the art of human relationships. Besides acting teachers and playwrights, other thinkers have defined human relationships: psychologists, anthropologists, historians, and economists. These theories often parallel theories about acting. The relative theory for Stanislavsky is *Freud's psychoanalysis.* Both place an emphasis on motivated and thwarted desire.

In Chapter 2 we'll fill in the rest of the chart: *the illusion of character, unifying image, suitable playwrights,* and *the intended reaction of the audience.*

Notebook: Getting to the Task

What follows is an example of how your notebook would look after several weeks of rehearsal if you were organizing the material into tasks and obstacles. The example is from *The Lesson*.

The actions are not
to question or *to answer*.
Those are paraphrases
of the activity.

The Professor's task? For this
you have to read the play. The
Professor kills the Pupil at the end.
That might be the Professor's
super-task, to teach the Pupil by
killing the Pupil.

The Pupil's super-task?
To be taught is passive, *to learn* is
better, but still not good. How about
to satisfy the Professor?

PROFESSOR Good. Let us arithmetize a little now.

PUPIL Yes, gladly, Professor.

PROFESSOR It wouldn't be too tiresome for you to tell me . . .

PUPIL Not at all, Professor, go on.

PROFESSOR How much are one and one?

PUPIL One and one make two.

If the Professor's task is
to kill the Pupil, the Professor's actions
will include tripping the Pupil up:
to flatter, to confuse.
(Notice that these all involve the Pupil)

PROFESSOR (*marveling at the* PUPIL'S *knowledge*) Oh, but that's very good. You appear to me to be well along in your studies. You should easily achieve the total doctorate, miss.

PUPIL I'm so glad. Especially to have someone like you tell me this.

PROFESSOR Let's push on: how much are two and one?

PUPIL Three.

PROFESSOR Three and one?

PUPIL Four.

PROFESSOR Four and one?

PUPIL Five

The Professor's actions are not
to praise (this is the activity): but
*to trap the Pupil, to inflate the Pupil's
ego, to stroke*

The Professor's actions can all change:
to strike, to whip, to flick, to dab

The Pupil's actions: *to slake,
to fend off, to avoid,* (not the
passive and intransitive *to respond*)

20

WHAT SHOULD I DO?

PROFESSOR Five and one?

PUPIL Six.

PROFESSOR Six and one?

PUPIL Seven.

PROFESSOR Seven and one?

PUPIL Eight.

PROFESSOR Seven and one?

PUPIL Eight again.

PROFESSOR Very well answered. Seven and one?

PUPIL Eight once more.

PROFESSOR Perfect. Excellent. Seven and one?

PUPIL Eight again. And sometimes nine.

PROFESSOR Magnificent. You are magnificent. You are exquisite. I congratulate you warmly, miss. There's scarcely any point in going on. At addition you are a past master. Now, let's look at subtraction. Tell me, if you're not exhausted, how many are four minus three?

PUPIL Four minus three? . . . Four minus three?

PROFESSOR Yes. I mean to say: subtract three from four.

PUPIL That makes . . . seven?

PROFESSOR I am sorry but I'm obliged to contradict you. Four minus three does not make seven. You are confused: four plus three makes seven, four minus three does not make seven . . . This is not addition anymore, we must subtract now.

PUPIL *(trying to understand)* Yes . . . yes . . .

PROFESSOR Four minus three makes . . . How many? . . . How many?

PUPIL Four?

PROFESSOR No, miss, that's not it.

PUPIL Three, then.

PROFESSOR Not that either, miss . . . Pardon, I'm sorry . . . I ought to say, that's not it . . . excuse me.

The Professor's obstacle:
The Pupil knows the answers
The Pupil's opportunity:
These questions are easy

The Professor's action:
to mask (own anger)
(Note: The Professor's action is not
to praise. That's the activity.)

The Professor's action: *to fool, to trick*

The Pupil's action:
*to stall the Professor, to keep
the Professor at a distance*

The Professor's action:
to push the Pupil
The Pupil's action:
to evade the Professor
The Professor's action:
to chase after the Pupil

The Pupil's action: *to grasp*
(not only the Professor's
meaning, but for help)
The Professor's action:
to close in on the Pupil
The Pupil's action:
to hide from the Professor

The Professor's action: *to pounce*
(Perhaps *not that either* is shouted,
which is why the Professor
apologizes later)

21

GETTING TO THE TASK

PUPIL Four minus three . . . Four minus three. Four minus three? . . . But now doesn't that make ten?

PROFESSOR Oh, certainly not, miss. It's not a matter of guessing. You've got to think it out. Let's try to deduce it together. Would you like to count?

PUPIL Yes, Professor. One . . . two . . . uh . . .

PROFESSOR You know how to count? How far can you count up to?

PUPIL I can count to . . . to infinity.

PROFESSOR That's not possible, miss.

PUPIL Well then, let's say to sixteen.

PROFESSOR That is enough. One must know one's limits.

The Pupil's action: *to distract the Professor,* not *to bluff* (that's the activity)
The Professor's action: *to unhinge the Pupil*

The Professor's action: *to mock* or
The Professor's action: *to torture*

The Pupil's action: *to rescue (self)*

The Professor's action: *to slam down on*

22

CHAPTER 2

THE IMPORTANCE OF OBSTACLES

In Stanislavsky's approach to performance, dramatic action happens when a performer tries to meet the demands of a task and an obstacle gets in the way. The through-line of a performance is a series of intersections between task and obstacle. It is this intersection that characterizes your role to the audience: they see you *choose* something else to do when your action runs into an obstacle. If you can't do one thing, then you choose to do another.

When you define character by obstacles, you don't define what you need, you define what you do when you don't get what you need. Cleverly trying another tack? Backing up, giving up, or smiling and deceiving other people? As in Freud's interpretation of behavior, emotion comes from the same intersection:

- I need this. I get it and I'm pleased.
- I need that. I don't get it and I'm annoyed.
- If I figure out a way to get past the obstacle, I'm pleased and satisfied.

In choosing tasks and actions, it is important to understand that they are most effective if they create a relationship with someone else—and they become especially interesting if they overcome an obstacle. Thinking about or striving for your needs is not the same as communicating or accomplishing your needs. The art of fulfilling your tasks will lead you to listen, to watch, and to respond sensitively to the environment, including the other people around you who have their *own* needs.

When onstage actions seem weak or passionless, the problem is usually that the obstacle onstage is too weak to challenge the actions to greater strength. It doesn't help to squeeze the task (or repeat the desperate acting teacher's command: *need it more!*), it helps to raise the obstacles. This is what spurs pole-vaulters to go higher. Coaches don't shout, "Jump higher, fool!" The bar to be jumped over is raised as an incentive for the pole-vaulter to go another tenth of an inch. Same thing here. To heighten the behavior onstage, challenge the action by making the obstacle *more difficult to overcome.*

But don't start with yourself; start with an active relationship. Every aspect of the rehearsal process, including investigating the meaning of the text, should involve creating a relationship with other actors. The fourteenth-century Japanese acting teacher Zeami wrote that every acting school has its secret. What is the secret song of an actor trained to accomplish tasks?

Sometimes I'm happy.
Sometimes I'm blue.
My disposition depends on you . . . (8)

Enlarging the Circle of Concentration

What you'll do in rehearsal is what Stanislavsky called **enlarging the circle of concentration**. The exercise is taken directly from a Raja Yoga practice. As you've read in Chapter 1, Stanislavsky was influenced by two schools of the Indian religious path called Yoga. He derived his relaxation and breathing exercises for actors from Hatha Yoga, which teaches meditation and relaxation through physical techniques. More applicable to our discussion of script analysis is Raja Yoga, which teaches that the mind observing itself can discriminate among its actions and, before it acts, can notice, respond, and achieve communion with increasing aspects of the world.

In practice, at every rehearsal you will consider new aspects of the production or your partner's ability to help or hinder your accomplishment of your task. Less noble than Yoga, we'll call it the Paranoid Theory of Acting. Everyone—and everything—onstage is either for you or against you. There's nothing neutral. Every aspect of the production should be included in the widening circle.

Now, of course you can't do that at once. Slowly, over time, you become increasingly sensitive to what's around you—not just noticing other people's and other things' presence, but letting their presence affect you. Today you're going to extend your concentration to the light, tomorrow to the other actor's hands, the next day to his neck, or his costume. This is a way to keep a performance fresh by discovering new ways to connect to the environment. Make a game of it if you like. At every rehearsal add one more thing to assign value as obstacle or opportunity.

Avoid extending concentration into the audience, though, or bang and bounce you'll go against the invisible fourth wall. Working strictly in this way, the task never, never, *never* involves the people in the audience. There are exceptions—even Stanislavsky had the actors enter through the audience for a production of Shakespeare's *Twelfth Night*—but these exceptions are rare. The illusion of a self-contained world is created by placing the actions and the obstacles on the stage.

The whole point is to create a real—not simulated—sequence of behavior onstage that is motivated by the given circumstances happening in front of the audience. Good acting is like good lying: tell 95 percent of the truth and you can slip in 5 percent that isn't the truth. Creating a relationship with someone else is so rare and so powerful that if you can do that for real, it's a lot easier to convince the audience, among other fibs, that you're sitting in Norway even though the audience is sitting in northern Illinois, ten feet away. The key to recreating a living truth on the stage: don't copy the form of truth; repeat the structure of relationships that got you to the truth. This is how twentieth-century acting theory and practice differ from what came before. In order to further understand Stanislavsky's contribution to the art of acting, it helps to know what came immediately before.

A Little History

Great acting—in the eyes of the beholder

Before we compare Stanislavsky's approach to acting to any approach that preceded it, it's important to recognize that long-gone acting is just that: long gone. Before the invention of the camera, audiences realized that the great theatrical performances they were witness to were precious, fleeting moments in time. They also recognized that great performances, like any great art work, somehow needed to be recorded and passed down to posterity as evidence of what the human spirit might achieve.

Yet, to try to fix a reliable portrait of "great" acting into words is as difficult as trying to capture the shifting appearance of the ocean's surface: what is being described keeps moving and changing. The descriptive words in the chronicles of acting throughout history likewise shift, their meanings relative to their time and place. When we read accounts of "great" performances—be they Eleonora Duse's or Bugs Bunny's—the same words appear, yet they are describing obviously different stories. The meaning of phrases such as "truthful emotions," "believably lifelike," and "natural" changes as rapidly and regularly as the ocean's waves; they have as fixed a meaning from century to century as the words "up-to-date." What is "believable" or "lifelike" depends on the beliefs and lives of the audience. An old saying goes that an actor's fame is written in water—or, as one actor said about himself, in hot water. Hot, cold, or tepid, that water keeps changing.

Nevertheless, behind the imprecise words that try to capture what is gone forever lies an undeniable passion. The writers trying to describe what they had witnessed on stage knew these performances were *already* gone forever. There is poignancy in that, and although we may not agree with or understand their assessments, we can't deny that they were moved by what they saw.*

We can also be curious about performances we would consider good that audiences of the past might have overlooked, or, having been blinded by their circumstances, not appreciated. In 1850, one of the first international stage stars in history, a dark-skinned African-American named Ira Aldridge, toured to Russia at the height of his fame to play Othello, Shylock, and Macbeth. The Russian actor Michael Schepkin, always credited as an earlier version of Stanislavsky because of Schepkin's eighteenth-century "realism," criticized Aldridge's calm and majesty in the role of Othello. Schepkin reminded Aldridge (who had won prizes for Latin composition in his youth) that Othello was a *Moor*: "hot southern blood seethes in his veins . . . he ought to rush at Desdemona and grab at her, and only then remember that he is a general and people are staring at him" (9). Schepkin's version might be realistic or not; it is certainly affected by his eighteenth-century vision of black people.

---

*Throughout this book, scenes from films are often used as examples of a performance. Film performances, of course, are the result of a team effort: the words can be dubbed, the mood manipulated by lighting or the musical soundtrack, the meaning of the performance rearranged by editing or computer graphics. Even so: when we watch a film performance, at least we can agree on what we're talking about.

In 1775, just before the American Revolution was about to start, a well-connected twenty-one-year-old girl made her London stage debut. Her married name was Mrs. Sarah Siddons, but she was better known in theater circles as the daughter of the celebrated Kemble acting family. Despite her connections, critics and audiences of 1775 didn't think much of Sarah Siddons, and she retreated to the provinces. Seven years later she returned to London and the same stage to be acclaimed as the greatest English actress who ever lived. Did Mrs. Siddons get better? Or did tastes change so that audiences appreciated what the actress had been doing all along?

When it comes to performances that date back to the time of George Washington, let's agree that we can't really know just what was "believable." Still, thanks to the distance of time, we can deduce a period's general trends. Again, as with the sea: there are calms, there are storms, there are tides. Before the rising tide of Stanislavsky's system, there were other systems of acting—classical and romantic—that, conveniently enough, can be remembered as a calm and a storm.

Classical acting

Classical acting was deliberately calm, though hardly calming. From letters, newspaper reviews, and engraved illustrations (which were as popular as baseball cards in their day), we can deduce that by the time the American Revolution was over and George Washington was President, Mrs. Siddons was London's reigning actress. Her younger brother, John Phillip Kemble, was the reigning actor-manager of Drury Lane, the same theater where Mrs. Siddons had her lackluster London debut and subsequent triumph. John was two years younger than his sister Sarah, and at the time of her debut he was off in a seminary studying to be a priest. Soon after, conveniently armed with a good working knowledge of Greek and Latin, he returned to the family acting trade.

Classical actors like Mrs. Siddons and John Phillip Kemble were concerned with posing and propriety. They stood on stage with dignity. They studied classical statues for ways to drape their clothes and to build their scenery. It was rumored they also copied their *gestures* from statues—why not imitate poses that would express emotion? In her spare time Mrs. Siddons sometimes sculpted, and her attitude toward her on-stage gestures was that of someone scrupulously concerned with graceful expression, carefully shaping the human form.

Classical acting was an approach of artful deliberation. It was lifelike—within its forms.* According to the tastes of the time, this meant balanced, stately movements and harmonious tones that were equally poised, balanced, and orderly—especially when expressing disorder. Once Sarah Siddons fainted onstage, something she did very believably in certain roles, but her audience knew it was for real and not an act because *they could see her legs*—which would never have been admitted to plain view if the lady was conscious. Of course, contemporary descriptions didn't say that. True to the discretion of the day, they referred to the sight of Mrs. Siddons's *uncovered limbs*.

---

*Stanislavsky called this kind of acting *representation*, because the performers *re-presented* their characters rather than embodied them.

THE IMPORTANCE OF OBSTACLES

We mustn't think that because legs couldn't be seen or spoken about directly that classical acting was cold—although it certainly was calculated. Mrs. Siddons was so emotional and convincing that other actors could choke up onstage when playing a scene with her. She herself was put out during her first tour to Edinburgh when, after one of her better speeches and effects, her Scottish audience failed to interrupt the scene with thunderous applause. Mrs. Siddons wrote in her *Reminiscences* that, while she was grateful for the silent appreciation, she needed time to breathe in order to work herself up for the next effect (10).

She wasn't being self-indulgent to expect a breather between bravos. The claptrap Mrs. Siddons was reciting was mostly rhetoric, and it required great gusts of wind. It was her practiced technique to draw energy and renewed concentration from a crowd's approval—unlike other actors, who would simply become distracted.*

This was one reason Sarah Siddons succeeded; her talent met the demands of the time. It also demonstrates that talent is a relative term. The ability to make love to the camera, for example, was not a recognized talent until film acting called for it. Turning pages of turgid rhetoric into thrilling stage events is no longer the necessary skill it was in Sarah's day, when actors were asked to say lines like:

Oh! give me daggers, fire, or water:

You can still view Mrs. Siddons's scripts, marked by her own hand in blue pencil, and the underlined words and phrases with which she wanted to "bring out" her "points" to the audience. This is what her book looked like. The scene is from *Venice Preserved*, by Thomas Otway (10).

Oh! give me daggers, fire, or water:
How I could bleed, how burn, how drown, the waves
<u>Huzzing and foaming round my sinking head</u>
Till I descended to the peaceful bottom
Oh! there's all quiet, <u>here</u> all rage and fury:
The air's too thin and pierces my weak brain;
I long for thick substantial sleep: <u>Hell! Hell!</u>
<u>Burst from the centre, rage and roar aloud</u>
If thou art half so hot, so mad as I am.

Notice, by the way, that two of the lines to be "brought out" describe actions so clearly that they could be confused with stage directions. Huzzing? Sarah Siddons and other trained actors of her time could do so much huzzing with lines like the above that playwrights wrote similar speeches to show off actors' talents—something we'll notice happening in other times and places as well.

In addition to acting, audiences, critics, and theater professionals of the period

---

*This was training, not instinct. Before Sarah was ten, she had turned tail to the wings after an audience laughed at her. Her mother took her by the hand to the edge of the stage, calmed the crowd, and Sarah started again (10).

wanted the old plays to be harmoniously balanced, too. Shakespeare's *The Tragedy of King Lear* became a little less tragic with the addition of a happy ending. To balance the horrors of *Macbeth*, new scenes incorporated singing fairies and dancing elves.

At its worst, classical acting became a collection of poses and vocal tricks. One hand on the breast, the other extended in gesture, classical acting was called by detractors "the teapot school," and its practitioners were said to spout. In 1804, the rage of the London season was a little spouter, a twelve-year-old boy named Master Betty. Yes, that really was his name.* Master Betty could act up a storm of classical gestures. He played Hamlet, Macbeth, and Richard III. While he was popular, Mrs. Siddons withdrew from the London season and went as far as Ireland for another tour. Her brother, on the other hand, had the good sense to book Master Betty while he was hot: Master Betty's Romeo took in more than double the Drury Lane's box office average (11). Master's Betty's star did wane, however, and Mrs. Siddons returned in force—sternly and nobly—to the London stage the next season.

Master Betty brushed aside, classical acting continued its calm reign in England, albeit briefly. It did go on to flourish in France, however, and in 1837 culminated in the person of a sixteen-year-old Jewish girl named Rachel. Actually, her name was Eliza Felix, but *Rachel* had more showbiz appeal than *Miss Felix* did. Rachel had been taught to stand like a statue and intone her lines with fever and passion. Far from being a monster like Master Betty, the teenage Rachel was acclaimed within months as a genius who excelled in high-minded, strong-willed princesses—Greek and Roman roles for which she could have had little life experience while strumming her guitar on the streets of Lyons where she had been discovered. Rachel's most successful role was Phaedra, a stepmother who lusts after her younger stepson. Rachel was twenty-two when she first played Phaedra; how old could the stepson have been? Fifteen? Where was Master Betty when they needed him? But Rachel's life experience didn't matter. She personified perfect forms, like a well-cut diamond. Don't think they didn't call her believable and lifelike. By the standards of the day, she *was*—and by any standards, brilliant.

Germany had its own classical acting, with rules laid down by the philosopher Goethe that decreed an actor must not only imitate nature, but present "her" ideally. That was Rule 35 (11). Other European countries had similar rules. It was considered very tasteful. People who didn't act "classically" were criticized for tastelessness.

Romantic acting

Romantic acting can be thought of as the storm after the calm. For all the success of classical acting, by the mid-nineteenth century there were people who wanted a little more life in their poses. The romantic literature, which had been tempered by the classical approach of what was sarcastically called the Kemble Religion, was now dispensed full strength (and then some) by actors of the romantic school. Romantic actors knew few rules of restraint. They believed poses should be less balanced, less poised, and less de-

---

*Master William Henry West Betty, to be precise. He made his debut at eleven, a year after seeing Mrs. Siddons in Belfast and declaring to his father: I shall certainly die if I do not become an actor!

liberate. An actor's poses should be, in theory, free to rise spontaneously from the performer's genius. Romantic acting, as with all romantic art, trusted that the soul of the artist would create its own evocative forms.

Edmund Kean was the British exemplar of this more dynamic style. When Mrs. Siddons was on tour in Ireland during Master Betty's flash in the pan, she played opposite an eighteen-year-old Kean. Did she recognize him from when he was eight? When Kean had been thrown out for misbehavior from a Kemble production of *Macbeth*—in which he played an elf? Within a short time—and for a short time—Edmund Kean was to become recognized around the world as a phenomenon of romantic acting, a style that maintained poses were formed by the personality of the performer, not by a rule of grace or the model of a statue. Kean executed some of the same roles that John Phillip Kemble had portrayed. The contrast was striking: the critic Leigh Hunt called it Kean's tears versus Kemble's cheeks of stone (12). Hamlet—a role Kemble had made moody and thoughtful—was played by Kean violently, his hands shattering the air in rapid and compulsive movement, his body trembling in fits and jerks, his voice ringing out in growls and roars. His listeners were awestruck; he was literally unnerving, his force of life so unbridled that audiences fainted at the sight and sound.

Don't think his gestures and poses were spontaneous. They were just as calculated as the ones derived from rules of taste. Kean counted the steps he took onstage, and complained that people thought he was making up what he took great pains to make appear spontaneous. When asked about the earnestness of a scene in which he choked another actor onstage, Kean replied, "In earnest! I should think so. Hang the fellow! He was trying to keep me out of the focus!" (13).

Athletic acting was the American contribution to all these poses. It's usually called by a fig leaf of a name—"heroic" acting—but perhaps "athletic" more captures what it was about. It was democratic as well: Adah Isaacs Menken, an African-American woman light-skinned enough to hide her racial background, was very famous for playing the male role of *Mazeppa*, galloping onto the stage on a "wild California mustang" and refusing to have a straw dummy double for her when it was time to be carried off upside down on the same horse. Wow.

Edwin Forrest was the greatest of the athletic actors. At eighteen, Forrest had played opposite Edmund Kean during Kean's American tour and was motivated to invent his own brand of over-the-top theatrics. Forrest's booming voice, fine physique, and horsemanship—he was bow-legged (which shows that "fine physique" is relative too)—made him wildly popular in America. He was less appreciated in England: when he played Macbeth in London, the audience hissed. Forrest always thought the British actor William Macready led the hissing. When Macready had the nerve to play his Macbeth in New York City, Forrest fans rioted in Astor Place. It may be inconceivable, but yes, they once cared about acting styles in America as much as they care about sports teams today.

The line between classical and romantic actors was hardly a fixed one. For example, Macready, who seems to have annoyed people in both camps, was criticized in classical quarters for performing with his necktie undone—as if he was in his own living room, complained the critic William Hazlitt (12). Whether their approach to acting was romantic or classical or some mix of the two, what actors using these approaches did was read a script and look for opportunities to illustrate the emotional state of their characters. The big question was which poses were better.

Melodrama

What happened to change all this posturing? The plays changed. As the theater became increasingly popular with audiences of different social backgrounds and education, *melodrama* became a dominant form. Today we think of melodrama as unrealistic because of its sensational situations (*the poor girl's house is on fire!*) and flat characters (*the bad man set the fire! the good man stopped it!*). To the audience of its day, melodrama seemed lifelike, realistic, and truthful, not least because the characters in melodramas began to include shop girls, sailors, and factory workers. It would be ludicrous for such down-to-earth types to roll on the floor, let alone copy a Greek statue. Posing seemed at odds with what these characters were saying, which required that they *did* look like they were spouting in their living room.

Did the subject matter of these plays invite the lower-class audience to attend the theater? Did the lower-class audience create a demand for plays that depicted lower-class people? A little of both. The excitements of melodrama compensated factory workers and clerks for their uneventful working hours. After a hard day at the factory, watching a play was easier than reading a book.

The hoi polloi had already been coming to the theater in Sarah Siddons's day. All too often on tour the cheaper seats would shout out: "Sally, me jewel, that's no bad!" Once when Mrs. Siddons was drinking the poison as Juliet, someone from the galleries yelled out: "Sip it up, lass!"* In order to satisfy the kind of spectator who didn't quite appreciate the nuances of a queen's hauteur or classical restraint—yet knew when a sailor or his girl was talking phony—melodrama required, before Stanislavsky's revelation of the importance of internal structures, a vocabulary of realistic poses to rival the gestures of classical or romantic acting. Called *naturalism*—the name is similar to that of a literary movement (more about that later)—this new style urged artists, including actors, to study nature.

Naturalism and naturalistic acting

The study of nature is an instinctive place to learn about acting. Making use of those observations, however, is a result of training. One of the first books of acting instruc-

---

*This happened in Leeds. The wit called out, in dialect: "Soop it oop, lass." At her curtain call, Mrs. Siddons said: "Goodbye, you brutes." Once again on a tour, this time to Scotland, the theater Mrs. Siddons was appearing at was so hot that the actress knew in advance she would be thirsty when she finished her Lady Macbeth. She asked that a beer be delivered to her at a certain time. The woman from her dressing room placed an order with the nearest tavern. The boy from the tavern arrived, hot on his task with a frothy mug, calling at the stage door for "Mrs. Siddons!" He asked a stagehand where the lady might be and the stagehand jerked his finger in the direction of the stage. Seizing the opportunity for a tip, the delivery boy walked onstage, mug in his outstretched hand, right in the middle of the sleep-walking scene. Mrs. Siddons proved an obstacle, and waved him away grandly, but he made an adjustment to ignore the meaning of her gestures and kept on coming until a stage manager ran out to grab both mug and boy. The lad was whisked off, with no chance to make a transition, his action thwarted, the task over, and the beer spilled. No tip, either (14).

tion in the English language, written in 1746, declares that observation of nature will produce a total of ten emotions in all (15). It recommends buying a three-quarter-length mirror, so that when the actor finds himself feeling one of the ten he can run to the mirror (three-quarter, not half) in order to make sure his forehead is smooth for joy or ruffled for anguish. Another acting treatise, written slightly later, points out that rolling eyes are the sign of quick wit in a man and loose morals in a woman (15). Observation, just as much as talent and truthfulness, depends on expectations.

A slightly more scientific approach to observation was taken in the 1840s by a Frenchman by the name of François Delsarte. Delsarte used to go to the park in Paris to observe people and take detailed notes about the ways happy people sat and sad people slumped. He had an eye for detail. He noticed that mothers who loved their children reached toward their child with the thumb lifted, and that hired nurses who were simply doing a job reached toward the child with the thumb turned inward. Delsarte made charts, too, which demonstrated the poses used for declarations of love and the grimaces of abject misery—along with notes, drawings, and schemes for the physical representation of other emotions. The original idea was to replace formulae by recording scientifically what could be found in nature. Delsarte's ideas, charts, and drawings became a formula of their own, of course—"naturalism."

Even with naturalism, one still analyzed a script to discover opportunities for effective poses and appropriate tones. The big question was the *source* of the gestures: copied from life, copied from statues, or free-form? This was not as zany as it sounds. Actors performing in a classical or romantic or naturalistic style were playing inside very large theaters. Any effective pose was welcome when one was entertaining houses that held over fifteen-hundred people—sometimes more than twice as much.* On those vast stages, in front of thousands of listeners, an actor's task involved speaking louder and clearer than in everyday life. Gestures had to be projected across the distance as well. Whether in broad daylight, lit by candles, or in the flicker of the gaslight that eventually illuminated the stage, performers needed to use big, bold shapes that could be seen and understood from afar—the visual equivalent of louder and clearer.

We can see the end of this style—the very tail end of it—in silent movies. The first professional silent movie actors were, for the most part, performers who had grown up with a vocabulary of familiar illustrative stage gestures. To avoid such mannerisms, the American director D.W. Griffith often used young actors with little if any stage experience; among them were the Gish sisters, Lillian and Dorothy. Lillian Gish said in an interview that she received her first and only acting lesson as a little girl: go out there and speak loudly and clearly so that everyone in the theater can hear you—*or they'll get another little girl who can* (16). Despite or because of their lack of more formal training, the Gish sisters' silent film performances are as nuanced, astute, and psychologically subtle as any ever since.

Watch their films and see for yourself. In *Orphans of the Storm* (1921), the sisters

---

*The size of stages expanded so much during Sarah Siddons's lifetime that she needed to enlarge her moves—make longer strides and slower turns, lead her movements from her hip, and move her arms more than she would have on a small stage. Siddons confessed to a friend that had she been starting out on such a large stage, her talent would have been lost.

play two orphans, one blind (Dorothy), one seeing (Lillian), separated by the French Revolution, the storm of the title. Throughout the film, the manner of acting is so understated and natural that whatever old-fashioned gestures remain stick out—you should pardon the expression—like sore thumbs. Sometimes the actors display overly-theatrical outstretched arms—silent film's equivalent to melodrama's cries for longing, mercy, or justice—but the scenario for *Orphans of the Storm* was adapted from an 1874 stage melodrama that included situations where outstretched arms would have been very effective onstage: for example, the cruelly separated sisters—one in a high balcony, the other on the street below—vainly reaching for each other.

More subtle and telling differences in approaches to acting in *Orphans of the Storm* can be noticed by paying attention to the close-ups in which different performers express the process of thinking. An experienced character actress, Lucille LaVerne, indicates her character's wicked thoughts with a malevolent side-long glance and a clenching fist to indicate "Gotcha!" The Gish sisters and most of the other actors do nothing of the kind and Griffith's camera records the genuine process of thought, as when Lillian's naturally wide eyes radiate delight, shock, understanding, or whatever else is on her mind.*

The Pioneers of Realism: Ibsen, Chekhov, Strindberg

Think of all the time that you've saved not having to study poses, copy Greek sculptures, or watch your forehead creasing in the mirror. Working to fulfil tasks, you'll try to create an inner dynamic structure that is active and changing, not fixed and static. Because of the nature of our medium—human relationships—we don't fix a formula of evocative forms. We believe inner emotion will lead to an evocative form, and we try to identify and reproduce the formula of the *inner emotion.*

Melodrama paved the way for realistic situations onstage and realistic plays, which, like the novels of George Eliot and Ivan Turgenev, dramatized interior action as much as outer action. The three pioneering authors who wrote plays that emphasized inner action and the drama of shifting relationships were from cold climates. Their names were infamous in their time but are celebrated in ours: Norway's Henrik Ibsen, Russia's Anton Chekhov, and Sweden's August Strindberg.

Could it be that these Scandinavian and Russian writers understood from birth the difference between a frozen outside and a burning inside? Maybe. Whatever the reasons, they created plays that required realistic and understated acting. Yes, they knew about each other. No, they didn't like each other, or each other's work. But they accomplished similar goals: they freed realistic plays from naturalistic formulae and presented the drama of the subconscious onstage. Within a short time of their writing, their plays revolutionized theater practices throughout the world.

The theater is notoriously the most conservative of art forms to digest new content. Because innovations in the theater cannot wait a hundred years in an attic before they are appreciated—because they must take place in front of a crowd—most innova-

---

*A transcript of Stanislavsky working with actors who are preparing a 1927 stage version of *Orphans of the Storm* appears in *Stanislavsky's Legacy*, translated by Elizabeth Reynolds Hapgood (Theatre Arts Books, 1958).

tions first suffer a baptism of uncomprehending fire. When Ibsen, Chekhov, and Strindberg started to create plays without clichés—texts that created the same internal drama that nineteenth-century novels did—critics and audiences were at first unready and unwilling to accept the change.

When Ibsen or Chekhov were performed in the typically large theaters in the accustomed style, it was often to disastrous reviews and dissatisfied audiences. Fortunately, understanding contemporary theater artists rose to these playwrights' challenges. Stanislavsky's inspiration, Eleonora Duse, excelled in roles written by Ibsen; they allowed her to demonstrate the best and subtlest aspects of her technique. Stanislavsky excelled in staging and performing Chekhov's work. Strindberg specifically called for a more intimate "chamber" theater where the behavior of the actors could be noticed in detail; he too had his champions and interpreters.

One of the first psychological dramas to achieve notoriety throughout Europe and America was *Hedda Gabler*, written by the self-exiled Norwegian, Henrik Ibsen. Nowadays one of the most admired plays in the repertory, *Hedda Gabler* was hissed and whistled down at its premiere performance on January 31, 1891, in Munich. Despite this initial reception, the play was quickly staged in other cities around Europe. Uncomprehending (and powerful) critics called Ibsen a "funereal clown." As to the play, Robert Buchanan of the *Illustrated London News* wrote: "For sheer unadulterated stupidity, for inherent meanness and vulgarity, for pretentious triviality . . . no Bostonian novel or London penny novelette has surpassed *Hedda Gabler*." "A bad escape of moral sewage-gas . . ." reported the *Pictorial World*. And *The People* concurred with "tedious turmoil of knaves and fools" (17).

The most indirectly perceptive of the negative critics was in Norway. Gerhard Gran, in *Samtiden* (1891) wrote:

> It is a law, or anyway has until now been a law, that drama, in its present state of technical development, can only present comparatively simple characters. . . . Everything that should make this curious being intelligible to us, her development, her secret thoughts, her half-sensed misgivings and all that vast region of the human mind which lies between the conscious and the unconscious—all this the dramatist can do no more than indicate. For that reason, I think a novel about Hedda Gabler would be extremely interesting, while the play leaves us with a sense of emptiness and betrayal (18).

Stanislavsky's technique, of course, was to release onstage just that "vast region of the mind between the conscious and the unconscious."

Organizing a Text for Its Obstacles: Rehearsing a Scene from *Hedda Gabler*

It seems appropriate, then, to use a scene from *Hedda Gabler* (19) as our example of how to organize a text for its *obstacles*. The play is named for its central character, the independent daughter of a General Gabler. After her father dies, Hedda marries the dull but well-meaning George Tesman. On her honeymoon Hedda realizes that her marriage is a mistake; by staying with her husband she is condemning herself to a living death as a trophy in a middle-class home. At the end of the four-act play she kills herself.

The scene we will look at is from the second act. Back from her honeymoon with Tesman, Hedda is meeting her old beau Mr. Løvborg for the first time since her marriage—and in her new home. Tesman is entertaining a guest of his own, Judge Brack.

HEDDA I'll keep Mr. Løvborg company a while.

TESMAN All right, Hedda dear, you do that.

> *He and* BRACK *go into the inner room, sit down, drink punch, smoke cigarettes, and talk animatedly during the following.* LØVBORG *remains standing by the stove.* HEDDA *goes to the writing table.*

HEDDA (*slightly raising her voice*) I can show you some photographs, if you like. Tesman and I traveled through the Tyrol on our way home.

> *She brings over an album and lays it on the table by the sofa, seating herself in the farthest corner.* LØVBORG *comes closer, stops, and looks at her. Then he takes a chair and sits down on her left, his back toward the inner room.*

HEDDA (*opening the album*) You see this view of the mountains, Mr. Løvborg. That's the Ortler group. Tesman's labeled them underneath. Here it is: "The Ortler group, near Meran."

LØVBORG (*whose eyes have never left her, speaking in a low, soft voice*) Hedda—Gabler!

HEDDA (*with a quick glance at him*) Ah! Shh!

LØVBORG (*repeating softly*) Hedda Gabler!

Examples of obstacles and opportunities

Let us agree that Hedda, like most people, would like to lead a fulfilled life. Her *supertask* will be *to escape from this marriage* and free herself from the strictures of social convention. One opportunity Hedda has to accomplish her task is this scene's visit from Mr. Løvborg. In the days before her marriage, when Hedda and Løvborg were close friends, Løvborg had been a hell-raiser. Hedda has heard that Løvborg is reformed, but she wishes it wasn't so. Could Løvborg rescue her from her prison? Why has he come to see her now that she's married?

Hedda's first *task* in this scene will be *to probe Løvborg's expectations.* Her first *action* will be *to overcome the obstacle of her husband* by putting Tesman at ease. Her manner in doing so will be shaped by another *obstacle*: she can be seen from the inner room as she sits with her old beau. The photo album gives Hedda and Løvborg some innocent-seeming *activity*; leafing through its pages is an *opportunity* to cover their actions.

THE IMPORTANCE OF OBSTACLES

In rehearsal, Løvborg's task, *to test whether Hedda still loves him*, meets the obstacle of Hedda's aloof cool as she seats herself in the farthest corner of the sofa and opens the photo album—without looking at him. The closeness of Tesman and Judge Brack are obvious obstacles to Løvborg, so his manner must be discreet if he is to speak with Hedda at all. Using the photo album, Hedda teases Løvborg, and perhaps baits him with the appearance of a happy marriage.

Løvborg's next action will be *to pierce Hedda's reserve*, to slice open her mask of contentment. His next actions will be determined by the obstacles that he encounters as he pursues her. He goes as far as he can before Hedda stops him. When he calls her by her maiden name, Hedda has gotten what she wanted: Løvborg has come to remind her of who she was before she married—Hedda *Gabler*, not Hedda *Tesman*. The sensuality of the scene is heightened by being *channeled* past obstacles.

Let's review the structure of the scene, which follows from Hedda's super-task of trying to *escape from this marriage*:

- task: *to probe Mr. Løvborg's expectations*
- obstacle: *her husband's kind attention*
- action: *to divert her husband*
- obstacle: *being seen*
- actions: *to mask* (herself), and then *to bait, to tease, to provoke Løvborg* until she gets what she wants and she makes a *transition* to the next task.

Note that Ibsen included stage directions that describe the activities:

HEDDA (*opening the album*)

LØVBORG (*whose eyes have never left her, speaking in a low, soft voice*)

HEDDA (*with a quick glance at him*)

LØVBORG (*repeating softly*)

HEDDA (*looks at the album*)

HEDDA (*turning the pages*)

LØVBORG (*resentment in his voice*)

HEDDA (*looks at him sharply*)

Ibsen had been a stage director in the relatively large city of Bergen and he understood that without such specific stage directions the actors and producers reading his script wouldn't understand what was happening in the scene. Even so, it was difficult for contemporary actors to interpret their roles in Ibsen's plays because the characters didn't declare their emotions as they did in melodramas. The stage directions in Ibsen are indications of inner actions and should be read as clues for motivation. *Why* does Hedda turn the pages? To tease Mr. Løvborg? Within the boundary of obstacles, Hedda has no other way to flirt with him. If you establish *to flirt* as the action, you might point at a specific mountain peak, rather than turn the page. Ibsen won't mind. In a letter to a young actress playing the heroine of *Rosmersholm*, the play he wrote before *Hedda Gabler*, Ibsen advised:

No declamation! No theatricalities! No grand mannerisms! Express every mood in a manner that will seem credible and natural. Never think of this or that actress whom you may have seen. Observe the life that is going on around you, and present a real and living human being (20).

Expanding the circle of concentration in rehearsal

The scene continues in this way:

> LØVBORG (*repeating softly*) Hedda Gabler!
>
> HEDDA (*looks at the album*) Yes, I used to be called that. In those days—when we two knew each other.
>
> LØVBORG And from now on—for the rest of my life—I have to teach myself not to say Hedda Gabler.
>
> HEDDA (*turning the pages*) Yes, you have to. And I think you ought to start practicing it. The sooner the better, I'd say.
>
> LØVBORG (*resentment in his voice*) Hedda Gabler married? And to George Tesman!
>
> HEDDA Yes—that's how it goes.
>
> LØVBORG Oh, Hedda, Hedda—how could you throw yourself away like that!
>
> HEDDA (*looks at him sharply*) All right—no more of that!
>
> LØVBORG What do you mean?
>
> TESMAN *comes in and over to the sofa.*

A quick list of Hedda's actions would include:

- to bait Løvborg
- to egg him on
- to tease him, yet to keep him at a distance
- to disguise her hurt

Every aspect of the production can be brought into the circle of concentration to help or hinder these and other actions. Begin with the setting. Tesman's Aunt Juju has decorated the room with overstuffed vases and Victorian furniture. The conventional décor is an obstacle to Hedda's need to escape; wherever she looks she is reminded of her new identity as an ornament. To Hedda, her home is a cage. Yet, if the light in the room is not bright, that is an opportunity for the two old lovers to sit close to each other using the photo album as a cover. There is also the opportunity to mask their feelings by leaning back into the shadows.

The sound of voices as the men smoke and drink in the inner room will be a constant obstacle, one Hedda and Løvborg will listen to actively. The smell of the men's cigarette smoke can also be included in the circle of concentration as one more aspect of the home's claustrophobic atmosphere. The clink of the punch glasses has the possibility to distract the teetotaler Mr. Løvborg, or to remind Hedda of her husband's unwanted presence.

If the production is accurate to the period (it doesn't have to be), Hedda will probably be corseted. Her tight dress will be an obstacle to any action. If she looks attractive in her costume, that will be an opportunity to arouse Løvborg and to charm her husband. The album, of course, is a world of possibilities. It is an opportunity for Hedda to sit next to Løvborg, and to bring her hand closer to his. She can bore her eyes into the album when her action is *to disguise her hurt*. She can point to its charmless photographs when her action is *to bait Løvborg* and mock her husband. The album is an obstacle for Løvborg, who would probably like to be talking about something other than Hedda's honeymoon with another man.

The specifics of the scene and its interpretation will naturally arise out of the relationship the two actors develop in rehearsal. If the actress playing Hedda is easily swayed by Løvborg, then Løvborg will be a different lover from one that Hedda can brush off. When Løvborg says, "Hedda Gabler married? And to George Tesman!" will Løvborg attack? Mock? Plead? The tone of the actress's response, "Yes—that's how it goes," will determine Løvborg's "Oh, Hedda, Hedda—how could you throw yourself away like that!"

The illusion of character is a web of relationships

If Hedda's behavior is molded by her dependence on other people and the environment, just what kind of person is she?

> LØVBORG Oh, Hedda, Hedda—how could you throw yourself away like that!
> HEDDA (*looks at him sharply*) All right—no more of that!
> LØVBORG What do you mean?
>
> TESMAN *comes in and over to the sofa.*
>
> HEDDA (*hears him coming and says casually*) And this one, Mr. Løvborg, was taken from the Val d'Ampezzo. Just look at the peaks of those mountains. (*looks warmly up at* TESMAN) Now what were those marvelous mountains called, dear?
> TESMAN Let me see. Oh, those are the Dolomites.
> HEDDA Why, of course! Those are the Dolomites, Mr. Løvborg.
> TESMAN Hedda dear—I only wanted to ask if we shouldn't bring in some punch anyway. At least for you, hm?
> HEDDA Yes, thank you. And a couple of *petits fours*, please.

In any acting technique, character is an illusion. You're not Hedda Gabler. You're just not. If you think you are, you should be in a mental institution, not on the stage. There is no such person, okay? It's a name on a page. You're an actor creating an illusion. The way you create the illusion of character for Stanislavsky—and the illusion of reality—is by *the web of active and dynamic relationships*.

Hedda is opposed in her tasks by all the characters in the play. That's what characterizes her. Tesman's Aunt Juju is suspicious of Hedda's fidelity and has installed a loyal maid to spy on the new wife. The neighbor, Judge Brack, is aware that Hedda chafes under the restrictions of convention and offers himself as a sexual diversion. But to Hedda, an affair with Brack would be only one more banality. The challenge for the actress is to make the dullness of the bourgeoisie such an obstacle to a fulfilled life that Hedda kills herself to escape it. When all the other characters act as obstacles to Hedda's task, they strengthen her character and the dramatic action of the play.

As the play develops, relationships shift. Hedda is pregnant as a consequence of her honeymoon (her corset will grow even tighter). The responsibilities of caring for a child will end any chance Hedda might have had to be an independent woman. Løvborg cannot save her; at a crucial time he fails her. Hedda's behavior in response to Løvborg grows so ambivalent that by the end of the third act she burns the manuscript for the book Løvborg has written, a book into which he has poured his life's thoughts. Løvborg's precious manuscript can be understood by the actress playing Hedda as competition for Løvborg's affections. Destroying the book destroys the obstacle of such a fascinating rival.

Tesman's concern for his wife is an obstacle of a different sort. It is a mistake when actors play Tesman as a joke because if Hedda cannot take Tesman seriously, the audience finds him dull, not funny. There is humor in his misplaced attentions only if they are heartfelt. To create the illusion of a realistic character, the actor playing Tesman must have an effect on Hedda. If he is deeply in love with his wife, that is an obstacle that will drag on her resolve to leave him.

Hedda is sly when she flirtatiously orders her husband out of the room for petit fours. She is also naïve enough to be cornered in Brack's trap, and romantic enough to try to rouse Løvborg to heroics. These relationships will be created in rehearsals and form a composition that changes in time. Again, the actress playing Hedda will not BE romantic or BE naïve. Her actions will create those changing qualities; the intersection of actions with obstacles will create her evolving emotions.

The analogy of oil painting

There is a parallel between Stanislavsky's technique of building a character and the illusion of depth in oil painting. In an oil painting, the artist puts down layer upon layer of paint. Beneath one layer the under-painting can be subtly seen. The effect of different layers viewed simultaneously is a sense of depth on the flat surface of the canvas. Similarly, in Stanislavsky's rehearsal technique, the dense layers of relationships between and among characters create the illusion of depth in an onstage role. Like the layers of oil paint, the layers of relationships take time to establish. A painter working in oil usually waits for one layer to dry before he puts down another. Likewise, in rehearsal the actor needs time to establish (and develop) each of the overlapping relationships.

For example, Tesman's task *to put his guest at ease* is an obstacle to Løvborg's task *to regain intimacy with Hedda*, yet it serves Hedda's action in deflecting Løvborg's attack on her façade. Ibsen was a master at writing scenes where different characters fulfil their chosen tasks even when they seem to be at odds. This is one of the ways in which Ibsen's work differs from melodrama; there is no agreed-on interpretation of the meaning of actions. There are only struggling ideas of what is right. It is exactly this moral relativism that made the Victorian critics identify *Hedda Gabler* as "moral sewage gas."

The sympathetic relationship with the audience

Although the character is an illusion, the emotions of the character are not. You experience real emotions onstage when you play your actions and attempt to accomplish your tasks. It is this, as much as anything, that Stanislavsky learned when observing Eleonora Duse. Inner conviction is so truthful it creates the illusion that what it speaks about is true. Genuine emotions onstage persuade the audience to sympathize with you.

Stanislavsky wanted his public to sympathize with characters. The actor's art, like the novelist's of the period, was meant to make the inner life of the characters available and emotionally resonant to the audience. As in the fiction written by Turgenev, Tolstoy, and Dostoyevsky, there are no villains or even heroes. There are only people who perform different actions for understandable—if not always shared—reasons. In his novel *Resurrection*, Tolstoy writes:

> One of the most widespread superstitions is that every man has his own special, definite qualities; that a man is kind, cruel, wise, stupid, energetic, apathetic, etc. Men are not like that. We may say of a man that he is more often kind than cruel, oftener wise than stupid, oftener energetic than apathetic, or the reverse; but it would be false to say of one man that he is kind and wise, of another that he is wicked and foolish. And yet we always classify mankind in this way. And this is untrue. Men are like rivers: the water is the same in each, and alike in all; but every river is narrow here, is more rapid there, here slower, there broader, now clear, now cold, now dull, now warm. It is the same with men. Every man carries in himself the germs of every quality, and sometimes one manifests itself, sometimes another, and the man often becomes unlike himself, while still remaining the same man (21).

With this in mind, it is important that the audience be sympathetic to Hedda's motivations as well as the motivations of her unwitting oppressors: her husband, his aunt, and the maid. Following Stanislavsky's dictum, even the amoral Judge Brack should be played for the basic humanity of his task. In his own mind Brack is trying to help Hedda as best as he can. Done well, the role of Brack can become a figure of pity to the audience because, in his ignorance, Brack knows no better than to frighten the person he would comfort. No matter what the role, the performance of action and obstacles is meant to elicit *compassion*.

Notebook:
Obstacles and Opportunities

HEDDA I'll keep Mr. Løvborg company a while.

TESMAN All right, Hedda dear, you do that.

He and BRACK *go into the inner room, sit down, drink punch, smoke cigarettes, and talk animatedly during the following.* LØVBORG *remains standing by the stove.* HEDDA *goes to the writing table.*

HEDDA *(slightly raising her voice)* I can show you some photographs, if you like. Tesman and I traveled through the Tyrol on our way home.

She brings over an album and lays it on the table by the sofa, seating herself in the farthest corner. LØVBORG *comes closer, stops, and looks at her. Then he takes a chair and sits down on her left, his back toward the inner room.*

HEDDA *(opening the album)* You see this view of the mountains, Mr. Løvborg. That's the Ortler group. Tesman's labeled them underneath. Here it is: "The Ortler group, near Meran."

LØVBORG *(whose eyes have never left her, speaking in a low, soft voice)* Hedda—Gabler!

HEDDA *(with a quick glance at him)* Ah! Shh!

LØVBORG *(repeating softly)* Hedda Gabler!

HEDDA *(looks at the album)* Yes, I used to be called that. In those days—when we two knew each other.

LØVBORG And from now on—for the rest of my life—I have to teach myself not to say Hedda Gabler.

Hedda's super-task:
to escape her marriage
Løvborg's super-task: *to rise again*

Hedda's task:
to see if Løvborg can rescue her
Løvborg's task:
to see if Hedda still loves him

Hedda's action:
to put Tesman at ease

Obstacle:
Hedda can be seen by Brack

Opportunity:
She can't be heard
if she speaks softly

Hedda's action:
to tease/to cover/to test
(Does he still love her?)

Opportunity (Hedda):
The album is an excuse
to sit close to Løvborg

Opportunity (Løvborg):
Hedda leaves room for
Løvborg on the sofa

Løvborg's action: *to test her*
(Is she still the same person?)

Hedda's action: *to bait*

Løvborg's action:
to pierce, to slice open

HEDDA (*turning the pages*) Yes, you have to. And I think you ought to start practicing it. The sooner the better, I'd say.

Hedda's action: *to egg him on*
Løvborg's action:
to lure her out of her cover
Hedda's action: *to tease him, yet keep him at a distance*

LØVBORG (*resentment in his voice*) Hedda Gabler married? And to George Tesman!
HEDDA Yes—that's how it goes.
LØVBORG Oh, Hedda, Hedda—how could you throw yourself away like that!

Løvborg's action: *to jab her*

Hedda's action: *to tickle him*

HEDDA (*looks at him sharply*) All right—no more of that!
LØVBORG What do you mean?

Løvborg's action: *to pierce her reserve (to mock)*

Hedda's action: *to disguise her hurt*

Løvborg's action: *to wake her up*
Hedda's action: *to slap him*

TESMAN *comes in and over to the sofa.*

Obstacle (Løvborg):
the husband arrives

Opportunity (Hedda):
the husband arrives

HEDDA (*hears him coming and says casually*) And this one, Mr. Løvborg, was taken from the Val d'Ampezzo. Just look at the peaks of those mountains. (*looks warmly up at* TESMAN) Now what were those marvelous mountains called, dear?

Løvborg's action: *to pounce*
Obstacle: Tesman's solicitude
Opportunity: Tesman's solicitude

TESMAN Let me see. Oh, those are the Dolomites
HEDDA Why, of course! Those are the Dolomites, Mr. Løvborg.

Hedda's action: *to divert Tesman, to show off to Løvborg*

TESMAN Hedda, dear—I only wanted to ask if we shouldn't bring in some punch anyway. At least for you, hm?
HEDDA Yes, thank you. And a couple of *petits fours*.

Hedda's action: *to mock Tesman*, but *to tease Løvborg*

Tesman's action:
to make them comfortable
(Ironically, he is the obstacle to their comfort)

Practical Tips for Working

Why rehearse?

You rehearse in order to identify which actions work to meet the demands of your task and which actions do not. At the end of the rehearsal, take time to write notes for yourself. You might identify tasks. At the next rehearsal, if you play actions to accomplish those tasks, you'll learn what obstacles you encounter from the other actors. If that doesn't work, you're going to find obstacles and opportunities by using a prop, or a costume, or the scenery, or something else physically present in the room—including the heat or lack of it. But you're always going to start with what the other people onstage are doing. The rehearsal process is meant to be interactive between you and the other actors.

Many people think a rehearsal process is a series of less bad performances. Their process is to criticize each rehearsal in order to eliminate more and more bad choices until, after painstaking attacks, the choices become stage-worthy. A rehearsal process need not be a savage removal of bad choices, but a steady build-up of good and better choices. During productive rehearsals you plant the seeds of what works, watch what flourishes, and encourage what is successful so that it can overtake what isn't. If you find something that succeeds, the chances are good you will abandon what doesn't. What does not help will often drop away naturally.

Use what's there first

At the first reading, always focus on the other people as much as you focus on the text. Always use the immediate circumstances: having the book in your lap, not knowing the lines, meeting the other people in the cast. That's all you may have, so make the most of it. Don't pretend you're doing anything but reading the play to each other. The presence of the book can be a tool in creating a relationship.

Listen actively—nothing is lost

Listen actively so that the words being spoken provoke a response within you. Don't be so concerned with picking up the cue or losing your place. This isn't a performance; it's an investigation. In some languages the word for *rehearsal* is the same word as *probe*. Your earliest responses in rehearsal are like pencil sketches. The historical process of rehearsal and of art (and of life, by the way) is such that all sketches build depth to your eventual choices, even if they are replaced later by more effective ones.

There is a wonderful book written by the psychologist of art Rudolf Arnheim on the subject of Picasso's mural *Guernica*. It contains all the sketches for the mural, from Picasso's first doodle—which is a composition study on a little scrap of paper—to photographs of the wall-sized painting in progress. During the time of *Guernica*'s creation Picasso explored its themes by finishing several other paintings with similar subject matter. The figure of a bull, for instance, received a lot of the artist's repeated attention.

Picasso sketched it as a cave drawing, as a wise Greek face, and as a realistic animal. Doing so, he learned for himself what the varying nature of the bull could be to him in his work. You will do similar sketches of your relationships in rehearsal.

Get your nose out of the book

End and begin sentences with your eyes on the other person, not on the book. This is because (presumably) the other person will have been listening and will have some reaction to what you say. The book will not have a reaction. It will lie there flat. From the beginning, you want to be in the habit of speaking with the purpose of creating and observing a response in the person to whom you are speaking. Don't take it for granted that the other person has had a reaction; take the time to notice it. Look up from the book not only to listen, but also to see the effect of what you've just said. *This is especially important if you get what you want.* See it. Don't assume it.

Use what you have around you, because that is truthful. Use that you're nervous or that the words are confusing. Again, as with good lying, acting is slipping in a few untruths among many truths.

Learn from Mae West (take notes for yourself)

Take notes for yourself; don't just record what the director tells you. As that lowdown 1920s vaudevillian turned glamorous 1930s movie star Mae West always said: *Keep a diary, girls, and one day it'll keep you.* It's true. All too often in rehearsal you see actors writing down the notes given to them by the director, as if they had no ideas of their own. Yes, performers are called actors, not writers, and their work should be done playing actions, not writing about them. Yes, it is true that to write actions down is to distort them by translating them into another medium. If you have the luxury of a long rehearsal period and not much else to think about during the long rehearsal period, you will not need to keep your own notes. If you're one of those people who remembers everything, you won't need to keep notes. Most people can risk the distortion of writing something down, and should use notes to organize themselves.

Should a director give you notes, you can write them down and translate them into your own structure of actions and obstacles. Suppose the director has something typically vague to relay like: "It's not interesting enough. Make it more interesting." What should that mean to you? That the director is bored? Don't panic and react by playing the action harder. No. Raise the difficulty of the obstacle. To increase the heat of the action and the size of your behavior, make the obstacle more difficult to overcome. Yes, look more deeply into yourself, in order to react to the other people onstage.

Learn from Bugs Bunny (go backward to go forward)

Before Bugs Bunny—the cartoon character who's as fast on his feet as he is with a quip—springs forward, he does a little preparation move backward. Think of yourself doing the same before playing an action. Take a moment to take in the situation. Your action will take place in order to solve a problem, or to enter an environment. Take the time to assess or be affected by the problem you are about to solve.

Work with an image

If you find that the task organizes itself around an image—an animal in a cage or a fox-hunt, for example—let that image provide a vocabulary for the actions: *to claw, to chase to the ground.* In another section of the book we will talk about organizing a text primarily with images, but here, let's recognize their power to refine the actions. Choosing the right word for a task is not meant to be a task in itself, as if an actor's work was to find the solution to a crossword puzzle, but the power of a word used to specify action will help you to specify your performance. You may find that once you've established the image you will go back and relabel the task.

For Michael Chekhov, the playwright's nephew and a member of Stanislavsky's first studio, the image for a task was always a "psychological gesture," a physical movement that summed up the super-task. For example, the Professor in *The Lesson* might compulsively ball his hands into fists. This could be very effective—and it wouldn't necessarily have to happen in performance or rehearsal. The gesture could remain most useful as a wordless way of specifying his super-task.

A sign of a good action is when you start to gesture as you try to find an apt word. That usually means the action is something you already do. Giving it a name clarifies it so that it is repeatable. When choosing a word or wordless images to organize your thinking, always remember to pick tasks that move you and excite you to act out the scene.

Work with the other actors

Should you tell the other actors your tasks? Should you ask them to play obstacles to increase the dramatic action of the scene? Unless you're paying the other actors' salaries, that isn't advisable. Even if you are paying their salaries, don't tell the other actors what to do. Let's put it this way: it's like making love. It works better (for most people) if you *do* it rather than talk about it. If your partner is doing something that arouses you, it's better for him to notice your response himself and increase or continue or cease what he is doing. It's probably better if there isn't much discussion about it, so that it remains physical, ambiguous, and changeable. As a lover, so as an actor. You could say a discreet *I like when you do that*, perhaps. There are exceptions: some people like to be told what to do. That doesn't mean they're going to do it. Acting is like any other partnership; you establish your own communication, in this case onstage.

The most celebrated partnership in cinematic ballroom dance, Fred Astaire and Ginger Rogers, didn't socialize together. They didn't even particularly like each other, which probably made their communication in performance and rehearsal all the more critical. Going into rehearsal, you hope that all your acting partners will have instincts and be sensitive to what the two or three or five of you are creating together. Once in a blue moon the director will help you define or refine what's going on between you, although more likely the director will be worried about the lighting.

THE IMPORTANCE OF OBSTACLES

What if the other actors aren't doing anything? The obstacle is that they are *no* obstacle. Well, that's not as bad as it sounds. It's worse when the other actors are doing too much. When they're not doing anything, you can endow them in your imagination with the ability to affect your behavior. Better yet, you can over-sensitize yourself to what they do. If you interpret every pause your partner takes as hostile, then the audience will project onto your partner the ability to affect you in that way. As in all perception, we understand the significance of something by the way it affects or relates to something else. If the other actors don't move you, pretend that they do. Channel your frustration with their wooden behavior into an active relationship with them.

What if the other actor does too much? There are so many obstacles that getting to an action that might further the task seems impossible. Learn from the masters: sit back. There is nothing so powerful as actively listening onstage and reacting. Look at Audrey Meadows as Alice in the classic television series *The Honeymooners*, how wonderful her performance is. It's Jackie Gleason's show, but Meadows is doing a remarkable job of holding her own with him. She doesn't do it by trying to top him; she goes underneath by having what he does affect her selectively. She doesn't respond to his large theatrics, she bides her time for something to be significant to her. This is also a good lesson for dealing with overly dramatic people in life. Let them have their little or gigantic fit. When they're out of breath, you can pounce.

The B choice (as in grade-B) is to attack and provoke the partner or group into some desired behavior. Let's call this the Sweaty Approach. It can be wonderful in rehearsal. It is rarely wonderful in performance. Usually it comes across as loud and intense. But mostly loud. The last resort of a sterile imagination and a dull way to avoid dealing with the other people onstage is to break the furniture or the props. It's like screaming: a little of it goes a very long way. It's better to hold back and let the possibility for violence act as a menace.

In a film, shouting, screaming, and throwing things can be made effective when such behavior is focused, selected, and edited. Onstage, more often than not, it's simply a wash of emotion. Even in a film—and with the best of actors—the results can still be lackluster. An example: one of the few dull sequences in the film *Citizen Kane* (1941) is when Kane tears apart the room after his wife leaves him. Off the set, Orson Welles, who was directing and playing Kane himself, scandalously tore apart a room at a restaurant. He decided to quote his shameful behavior in the film. The crew preparing to shoot the scene were shocked that Welles would use his own private life so openly. A room to be destroyed (with mirrors!) was set up, cameras were safely placed, and self-referential Orson went in there and tossed the chairs around. As exciting as this may have been on the set, in the film the sequence is uninvolving. After the first two seconds we don't need or want to see or hear the rest of the scene. Orson Welles acting with the furniture is simply not as engaging as Orson Welles acting with people.

Don't toss people around onstage, either.

Of course, not everything in the environment is going to be an obstacle. There will be opportunities to further the tasks. Opportunities are less dramatic than obstacles onstage, unless they come after a long series of obstacles. Turning an obstacle into an opportunity is always an appealing choice, but the script will not always allow this to happen.

The Chart

Near the end of Chapter 1 we reviewed the chart that compares five different ways of organizing and analyzing a text. There are four more categories: the *illusion of character*, the *unifying image*, *suitable playwrights*, and the *intended reaction of the audience*.

- **The illusion of character.** The illusion of depth in a drawing is most simply created by placing one figure over another. The illusion of depth in a character is created by different means. For Stanislavsky, a *web of relationships* between people creates the illusion of character on stage.
- **Unifying image.** Building a role in rehearsal by overlaying relationships among characters is similar to the process of an *oil painting*, where depth is built up with layers of paint.
- **Suitable playwrights.** Different approaches to organizing a text are appropriate, though by no means limited to the work of certain authors. Although Stanislavsky would never have limited his Stanislavsky System to specialize in or exclude any one form or style, the approach, with its emphasis on the illusion of reality, is particularly appropriate for those realistic playwrights like *Chekhov, Strindberg,* and *Ibsen*. Paradoxically, it also works well for absurdist playwrights like *Ionesco, Beckett,* and *Pinter,* where an inner logic organizes the behavior of the roles.
- **The intended reaction of the audience.** It was intended by Stanislavsky that his audience have *compassion* for the actions of the actors. No character should be seen as a villain or a hero, but only as a human being with recognizable hopes, dreams, and ambitions with which the audience can identify.

CHAPTER 3

STANISLAVSKY'S LEGACY

Konstantin Stanislavsky stressed that his system was a basic vocabulary. He applied it to melodrama, opera, realistic plays, and stylized verse plays written by Shakespeare and Molière. He insisted that, although it came from Russia, his system was applicable to all the stages of the world. Time has shown he was right. Russian émigrés would teach the Stanislavsky System in New York and Hollywood, in London, in Paris, and in Beijing.

Stanislavsky in Russia

When Stanislavsky died in 1938, he was seventy-five. He had been born in Russia under an all-powerful Tsar, two years before the freeing of Russia's serfs. During his lifetime his country passed through a revolution whose leader, Vladimir Ilyich Lenin, held out the hope, justified or not, that there would be freedom for all in the new Soviet Union. In the last fifteen years of Stanislavsky's life, Russia regressed under the rule of a latter-day Tsar, Josef Stalin, who studied Ivan Grozny for ways to subdue his own countrymen (remember Repin's painting?).

In Stanislavsky's youth, his father was rich enough to build and equip an amateur theater on their family estate; after the Revolution, the family property was confiscated by the government. Despite his later success onstage, Stanislavsky was desperately poor and hadn't money enough for decent clothes or his own son's tuberculosis treatments. The minister of culture appealed to Lenin that Stanislavsky was down to his last pair of pants. Fortunately, Lenin had seen and enjoyed Stanislavsky's performances, and authorized the government to give Stanislavsky a small house with two rooms to rehearse in.

Adaptation

The humanism of Stanislavsky's work and its accessibility fit in well with the Soviets' task of bringing art called *Socialist Realism* to the masses. Socialist Realism is an approach to art dedicated to the display of positive role models. It takes as its mission the inclusion of groups that have not previously been represented or active in art, especially the lower classes. It is also meant to invite those previously excluded groups to participate in art as creators and enthusiasts. It emphasizes realism because it assumes realistic art is most accessible to all groups.* The Itinerant painters, depicting criminals on the way to Siberia, or revolutionaries passing out pamphlets, fit the bill and were marched into Soviet art history as prophetic predecessors.

Stanislavsky's Soviet "protectors" made sure Socialist Realism became the *only* approach to art—including the art of acting—permitted by the all-powerful government. Stanislavsky somehow came to terms with the new regime. Sometimes he merely misunderstood what was going on, or lived blissfully ignorant. He did use his position to do good. When radical artists were attacked for not making their work accessible enough, Stanislavsky did what he could to shield them with his prestige. True, in many cases it made no difference, but he made public efforts when it was dangerous for him to do so. In *An Actor Prepares*, Stanislavsky illustrates an actor's technique of adapting to circumstances with an example so revealing in its specifics that it would lose its meaning if it were simplified or paraphrased. Here is the quote:

> "Suppose that you, Kostya, hold some high position and I have to ask a favor of you. I must enlist your aid. But you do not know me at all. How can I make myself stand out from the others who are trying to get help from you?
>
> "I must rivet your attention on me and control it. How can I strengthen and make the most of the slight contact between us? How can I influence you to take a favorable attitude toward me? How can I reach your mind, your feelings, your attention, your imagination? How can I touch the very soul of such an influential person?
>
> "If only I can make him conjure up a picture in his mind's eye that in any way approximates the dreadful reality of my circumstances, I know his interest will be aroused. He will look into me more attentively, his heart will be touched. But to reach this point I must penetrate into the being of the other person, I must sense his life, I must adapt myself to it." (22)

Towards the end of his life Stanislavsky was a respected figure of culture who had known other respected Russian figures of culture to be arrested, jailed, or executed. As with other prestigious artists who were elderly, Stanislavsky was surrounded by nurses and attendants who screened him from the world. In the last few years of his life, it seems Stanislavsky was under virtual house arrest.

The Story of the Book

In line with Stalin

There was sustained pressure on Stanislavsky to align his system with Communism, but his system had always been playfully contradictory, choosing to emphasize one aspect

---

*It isn't always.

and then another of union between body and mind, guided by the practices of Yoga and reinforced by the psychological theories of Théodule Ribot that motion could produce emotion and vice versa. The Soviet government wanted acting theory, and any other theory in the land, to be a clear, rigid, and unified set of rules—and not ever vice versa. Soviet thinking held that all behavior was determined by physical circumstances, not by thoughts. Knowledge of Freud was derided or suppressed and any aspect of Stanislavsky's system that unknowingly paralleled that theory was held suspect as subversive. Talk of Yoga, or any mystic religious practice, was probably even worse in aggressively atheist Soviet Russia.*

Revisions

One of the prices Stanislavsky paid for survival in this environment was extracted when his first book was adopted as a textbook for model Soviet theater schools. This meant the book had to be approved by Communist censors and, when it deviated from the prescribed path, brought back in line. In 1928, Lyubov Gurevich, a woman who had been Stanislavsky's literary advisor for over thirty years, warned Stanislavsky to avoid references in his book to Ribot's affective memory and to become more aware of the claptrap that passed for psychology in Stalin's Russia.† She had a point. Among other terms the censors objected to: the spirit, the soul, intuition, and the subconscious. Out, of course, went the references to Yoga that ran throughout the text, including key Hindu words like *prana* (the Yogic concept of vital energy) and *chakras* (the bundles of concentrated energy within the spine). Stanislavsky responded with supple adaptation; words may have changed, but he held to his key concepts. The government urged teachers who worked from the book to emphasize its physical exercises and ignore the half concerned with psychology. If, at the end of his life, Stanislavsky also stressed the physical side of his theory, perhaps it was his way to make peace with his captors.

Stanislavsky's death provided the Soviet commissars with an opportunity to bronze his quicksilver thought into an unyielding doctrine, something it had never been in his lifetime. Until the end his mind was flexible. In his last work with actors, held in his home, he abandoned table talk for active rehearsals. He was preparing a production of Molière's *Tartuffe*—not a realistic play, but one in verse. Three months before he died, he told his directing students: "One must give actors various paths. One of these is the path of action. There is also another path: you can move from feeling to action, arousing feeling first" (23).

---

*Eastern religions were particularly threatening to the Soviet Union because they had the potential to encourage the Eastern countries under Russian control to establish separate national and ethnic identities. Beginning in the 1920s, and continuing into the 1930s, the Communist government went out of its way to suppress and humiliate Eastern thought, going so far as to make sure it was publicized that a hippopotamus was dissected inside a famous Buddhist temple in Saint Petersburg—a gross sacrilege for that sect.

†Stanislavsky had never graduated from school and felt the need for more book learning. Lyubov Gurevich advised him. Throughout Stanislavsky's life, she urged to him write books of his own and looked out for him in other ways as well.

The Story of the Theater Claimed for Him After His Death

In 1897 Stanislavsky formed a theater company with Vladimir Nemerovitch-Danchenko, a Russian writer, educator, and producer. The troupe was called the Moscow Art Theater. In Russia, the company is known by its initials as MXAT and called in Russian *Moohat* (accent on the second syllable, the *h* slightly breathy). MXAT's aim was to improve the standards of Russian theater and bring it in line with what has since been called the Silver Age of Russian arts: a rebirth of the spirit in literature, dance, and painting.

Stanislavsky's MXAT performances as an actor were riveting to his audiences, especially his portrayals of Dr. Stockman in Ibsen's *An Enemy of the People* and the difficult title role of *Othello*—the latter being Stanislavsky's homage to his idol Tommaso Salvini. Stanislavsky had no system of working as an actor when the Moscow Art Theater was founded, and he only began to search for a system after his successful performances of Dr. Stockman began to lose their power.

Neither the actors of MXAT nor Stanislavsky's partner were eager to use the techniques Stanislavsky discovered. But by 1911 Stanislavsky had become so certain of his techniques that he threatened to quit if they weren't adopted by the company. The actors agreed, for a year, then chafed under the discipline of having to learn what they termed "eccentric." Eventually, Stanislavsky went outside MXAT to create a studio where he taught and worked on his system more systematically.

Still, it was while working at the MXAT that the Russian pioneer of psychological realism in acting found the ideal vehicles for his explorations—the psychologically realistic plays of Anton Chekhov. Stanislavsky learned from staging and acting in long-running, critically acclaimed productions of Chekhov's *Seagull* and *Uncle Vanya* even before his system was in place. These popular productions, after disastrous earlier versions at more established theaters, made MXAT's—and Chekhov's—reputations. Chekhov wrote two other plays specifically for MXAT, *The Cherry Orchard* and *The Three Sisters*. MXAT was also where he met the company actress who would later become his wife.*

Although these productions had been created without Stanislavsky's system, Stanislavsky toured the world with them as examples of his work. The tours, beginning in 1906, brought awareness of the achievement of Stanislavsky's approach to acting to France, to Germany, and, on an especially fateful tour in 1923, to America. There were other plays in the repertory by that time that had been created using his system, but as Stanislavsky put it: "America wants to see what Europe already knows" (23). Stanislavsky toured America for two years, during which his company gave three-hundred and eighty performances, with special matinees on Fridays so theatre professionals could attend.

Stanislavsky in America

Stanislavsky's American tour was performed in Russian, of course. In the history of acting, the observation of foreign performers has often had powerful consequences. Re-

---

*It was also where his nephew Michael Chekhov would later work.

member how Stanislavsky was inspired by watching Duse and Salvini perform in Italian? It is no accident that he learned by watching foreign actors acting in a language he didn't speak. Without the distractions of such technical considerations as diction, accent, volume (up to a point), and, most importantly, the information value of the words, an audience watching a foreign language performance must concentrate on the relationships and reactions of the performers. To understand a foreign language, we very often gain meaning by seeing what effect the speaker has on other people. Duse and Salvini performed in Italian while the actors they were performing with spoke English. Ira Aldridge performed Othello in English while the actors around him spoke German or Russian or Polish, depending on the country they were in. The experience of watching operas performed in foreign languages had taught European audiences to enjoy onstage action without regard to the unknown (or unclear) words issuing from a singer's throat. American audiences in 1923 had experience watching silent films and had learned the habit of paying attention to behavior separately from any spoken language. The American audience's inability to understand Russian freed them to focus on and appreciate the nuances of psychological realism.

The Teachers

Eight days after MXAT opened in New York,* the first lecture on the subject of the Stanislavsky System in America was given by Richard Boleslavsky, an original member of the MXAT company who had left for America four years earlier but had been pressed into service for the MXAT tour. His was the accent that began the *beets/beads/bits* disagreement—and much else besides, depending on the expectations of the listeners.

Sitting in the audience at that lecture were Lee Strasberg and Harold Clurman, who were to become two of Stanislavsky's foremost disciples in America. Strasberg and Clurman took classes at the American Laboratory Theatre, where Boleslavsky taught in New York with another MXAT alumna, Maria Ouspenskaya. (She too had an unforgettable accent that, during the 1940s, would land her lucrative jobs in Hollywood B-pictures.)†

Clurman studied with Boleslavsky, Strasberg more often with Ouspenskaya. Boleslavsky's group, which also tried to produce plays, lasted until 1930, when it collapsed financially—despite the producer mortgaging her house and the actors providing weekly sums of money. A year later Clurman and Strasberg formed their own company, the Group Theatre, which also staged shows commercially. The Group Theatre began informally with Harold Clurman's Messianic post-performance lectures inside Broadway theaters on Friday nights. In the summer the company left the city and lived communally in the country. After rehearsals, the eager Americans would gather to listen as their cook (!), who knew Russian, would read out loud to them from Russian actors' diaries and theater history related to Stanislavsky.

The Group Theatre modeled itself on MXAT, cultivating socially aware play-

---

*January 18, 1923, at the Princess Theater.

†*The Wolf Man* (1941), *Frankenstein Meets the Wolf Man* (1943), *Tarzan and the Amazons* (1945).

wrights like Clifford Odets, whose first great success, *Waiting For Lefty* (1935), dramatized a labor strike. Sympathetic to the many people whose lives were ruined by the Depression—but ignorant of what was really going on in Russia—Group members flirted with Communism. Innocent that they were echoing Soviet censors, they insisted the plays they staged have upbeat endings. Before they demanded a change, Odets's play *Awake and Sing!* was originally titled *I Got the Blues.* Harold Clurman's book about this era sums it up in its title: *The Fervent Years.* Fervently, the members of the Group Theatre believed that by discovering Stanislavsky they had discovered a new way to live. More significantly, they had discovered a link between theater craft and the technique of Freudian psychoanalysis.

The Link with Freud

Freud's ideas were gaining legitimacy in America at this time, and the Group Theatre tried to combine the two similar interpretations of behavior. Freud's theories of repression seemed especially applicable to an actor's craft, and removing repression from an actor's subconscious seemed an obvious way to expand the emotional range of performing artists. The Group Theatre developed exercises to improve access to emotional memories hidden by repression. These became a specialty, and in time playwrights would include a speech or so in their plays to tap into the ability of actors to recall their past. Some talented and intuitive actors felt they were unsuited for their trade because, no matter how hard they tried, they were unable to mine their psyches for repressed emotional memories.

American arguments

In 1934 a key member of the Group Theatre, the actress Stella Adler, tracked Stanislavsky down in France. She first said to him, referring to the burden of emotional memory, "I loved the theater until you came along. And now I hate it!" (23). Stanislavsky wrote to a friend that Adler had been pestering him (she reports herself as being shy), but he felt sorry for her, and so, in his words, he wasted a month working with her. In all, Adler and Harold Clurman, to whom she was married at the time, spent six weeks with Stanislavsky discussing the American developments of his system. At the time, Stanislavsky was involved with the later, more physical developments of his approach that would be emphasized in Russia. He was to die four years later.

Adler returned to New York and announced that the Group Theatre had gotten it wrong—there was too much emphasis placed on emotional memory and uncovering repression. And it was *bits*, not *beats.** But Strasberg said that he preferred his interpretation—it was a method that got results, and he called it just that: "the Method."

Strasberg insisted the emphasis on emotional memory developed Stanislavsky's ideas. Adler thought otherwise; she had learned from Stanislavsky himself that fantasy

---

*She asked the wrong person. It was Boleslavsky who had said the word *bead.*

was just as potent as memory, and emotional memory was a dead end, not a route to a performance. Of course, she didn't consider why Stanislavsky might have told her that. When she had her conversations with him, the concept of emotional memory was suspect in Russia and dangerous to talk about.

It wasn't that Strasberg had gotten it wrong, or Stanislavsky had changed his mind—as Strasberg accused—but that Stanislavsky's thinking had shifted to emphasize another aspect of the same basic idea that emotion and motion were linked. The discussion of emotional memory was a non-issue in Russia, where teachers were working through their notes from the last of Stanislavsky's developments in physical acting.

Stanislavsky training in America split into two camps. Strasberg continued to emphasize the earlier part of the training, Adler kept Stanislavsky's later emphasis on a method of physical action, which included actors improvising the story of the play before any line analysis or investigation of psychological tasks—much less memories.

The Books—Lost in the Translation?

The field of Stanislavsky studies has cracked open with Sharon Marie Carnicke's startling discoveries that were set off in 1978 when she was serving as interpreter for a MXAT director working with Strasberg-trained actors in New York and she personally encountered the obstacles of American and Russian mutual misunderstanding.* One of the reasons such misunderstanding exists is the history of Stanislavsky's books. The story that follows is from Carnicke's *Stanislavsky in Focus*, as important a book in Stanislavsky studies as the original edition of *An Actor Prepares*.

The reason for the rights

In the late 1920s, Stanislavsky had a heart attack. He was in his sixties by then, and like many teachers facing death, before and since, he decided to put his notes in order. Because Communist Russia held property in common—including an author's royalties—Stanislavsky would have made no money if his book was published in Russia. So he decided to have the first version published in English and in the United States, where he had made money on his autobiography.

He invited Elizabeth Reynolds Hapgood to become his translator. Her husband, Norman Hapgood, was a theater critic, but Reynolds Hapgood herself initially knew little about the theater.† She had been Stanislavsky's interpreter at the White House—an odd job, considering protocol at the time held that foreigners could speak to the President only through an ambassador. In 1923, Soviet Russia was unrecognized by America and so had no ambassador. Therefore, Stanislavsky was not allowed to speak with Calvin Coolidge—although he did pose for photos.

---

*Strasberg himself would whisper critiques.

†One of the few non-émigré Americans at the time who could read and write Russian, Reynolds Hapgood founded the Russian Department at Columbia University.

Elizabeth Reynolds Hapgood must have made a good impression during her photo opportunity, because not only did Stanislavsky ask her to translate his books, he awarded her the rights in all languages in all countries for all time. Because Stanislavsky was irritated by the task of combing through many years' accumulation of contradictory notes—he'd been scribbling to himself about acting since he was fourteen years old— he urged Reynolds Hapgood not only to translate but to cut, edit, and rearrange; in essence to do anything to get the manuscript into shape. She took him up on the offer. Even so, it took her so long that after five years there was still no finished book. The original publisher withdrew.

Another American publisher offered to publish the first half of the unfinished manuscript, and in 1936 the book came out in America under the title *An Actor Prepares*. Reynolds Hapgood was under intense pressure from the new publisher to cut even this first half of the repetitive manuscript. She held out as best she could, but, perhaps less experienced than Stanislavsky facing his Russian censors, she did make cuts, some of substance.

The differences

As in Russia, gone were most direct references to Yoga—the publisher felt that Yoga didn't appeal to "Anglo-Saxons." Other changes were made, some big, some small, some as the result of requested cuts, but some also due to Reynolds Hapgood's free hand at interpretation. The key concept of *tasks*—which Reynolds translated as the word *objectives*—became, in America, the most commonly used term for speaking about Stanislavsky's system. Yet the word obscures the essence of Stanislavsky's approach: that acting is something you *do*. You can't do an objective. You can't attempt an objective. An objective is the goal. The Russian word for "objective" is very different from the Russian word more commonly translated as "tasks" or "problems."

Where did this word *objective* come from? At the time of this writing the link is unproved, but even a quick glance at the vocabulary used in the 1930s—and still used—to explain Raja Yoga in English reveals word clusters like "the object of desire" and statements that the conscious mind "acts in order to grasp the objects" (24). Other familiar word clusters occur in Raja Yoga literature: "hindered by obstacles," "analyze your thoughts," "scrutinize your motives." Perhaps the word *objective* is transmuted from this source, and the Yogic principles of Stanislavsky are woven deeper into the American translation than previously known or admitted.

There are other changes in *An Actor Prepares*, large and small. The published American book is 295 pages, while the published Russian that it purports to be translating is 575 pages! The manuscript in Russian, by the way, is 700 pages. Yet, legally, the English is the only authorized and easily accessible version. Legally, the extra 175 pages in Russian exist like hovering ghosts, prevented from translation by a vigorously enforced protection of the American copyright. Attempts to translate from the Russian original have been thwarted not only in America, but in Italy, Japan, and France. In 1954, when someone pointed out the differences in the texts, Reynolds Hapgood had a friend who had been a MXAT actress write an article defending the translation, and the American publisher went so far as to have a comparison made and a notarized statement issued that nothing important had been eliminated! The copyright is still held in America, although soon enough the Russian manuscript will be in the public domain and new translations might be published.

The gap between Russia and America

The Reynolds Hapgood version, whatever its connection to Stanislavsky, has nevertheless shaped understanding of Stanislavsky in America. In addition to the differences in the text, there is also the matter of the title, *An Actor Prepares*. Stanislavsky's original manuscript grew so large it split into two parts. He reluctantly agreed to have the first half published separately. The book's Russian title could be translated as *An Actor's Work on Himself, Part One*. At the insistence of the publisher, the American title was made to seem complete—the result being that the teachings of Stanislavsky in this county derive only from the first half, without anyone being told there was more.

In 1948, ten years after Stanislavsky's death, a second book came out in Russia. The next year a book was issued under Stanislavsky's name in English, called by Reynolds Hapgood *Building a Character* (1949). Although it gives the appearance of a unified whole, *Building a Character* is made up of different articles from a span of twenty years. A third book published in America called *Creating a Role* (1961) is even more divergent from any Russian source. Joshua Logan, who wrote the introduction to *Creating a Role*, reports in his biography that Stanislavsky said to him, "Oh, I see you've read my books. Well . . . . We have extended past that. Now that's for the bathroom" (25). There is no Russian word for "bathroom," not in the English sense, and Logan's translator was being polite. What Stanislavsky said was more properly translated: "Now that's for the toilet."*

The American identity of Stanislavsky was further sealed off from Russia by the Cold War isolation between the two countries. Although Stanislavsky's system changed over time, the instructors who were in America to teach it were early Russian émigrés who had no further contact with their native country—at least regarding acting theory—and so taught the early version they had learned with its emphasis on sitting around the table. Later developments in Russia went unnoticed and untranslated.

"The System" or "The Method"?

American understanding of Stanislavsky has thus been shaped by willfulness and political reality, linked to a psychology Stanislavsky would have been arrested for had he ever discussed it. The interpretive abridged American translation of Stanislavsky's writings, the opportunity to create an independent way of thinking during the publication gap between the first and second volumes, the reluctance of professionals to revisit their

---

*"Banya" is the Russian word for "bath." The Russian word for "toilet" is—"toilet."

basic training—all these helped to create a new identity for Stanislavsky's system until it became, in America, indistinguishable from Lee Strasberg's "Method."

In addition, an entire set of jargon has evolved, added by various teachers: not just "objectives" but also "intentions," "indicating," and "beats." Strasberg's knowledge of Stanislavsky was genuine; working from an unauthorized German translation,* he taught the basic principles of desire and obstacles at the Actors Studio—the school he was initially excluded from but eventually took over. The students who emerged from the Studio, many of them popular and influential, assumed they were receiving Stanislavsky training, and, in the essentials, they were.

Among certain performers, however, the Method, which was initially meant to root out acting styles, became an acting style itself, and the popularity of that style—like Delsarte's attempts at "naturalism"—created its own bouquet of poses: the grunt, the yawn, the yearning pause. Stanislavsky himself had talked about "stencils" of such behavior. When old-fashioned Russian actors played peasants, they spat on the floor for "realism." In the place of classical or romantic poses, the Method substituted psychological poses and prompted endless discussion in rehearsal about motivation.

The Method was so popular that it invited attack. There are many anecdotes told about the old-style hams meeting the new-style narcissists. The emphasis on motionless action seemed like the emperor's new clothes, and the chapter of *An Actor Prepares* in which an actor is asked to be a tree became a surefire joke. The period excesses of Method acting claiming to be derived from the Stanislavsky System can be seen in 1950s television and film performances, where scratching, grunting, and other details of *verismo* are the studied clichés of "acting naturally." When it works, however, Method acting can be glorious, especially in film, where the technical skill of Method actors allows for great sophistication.

Application in Film

The link between Stanislavsky and America is not only personal. The demands of American film (and later television) for realistic acting gave the Stanislavsky System great opportunities for application. Look at the performances in the 1951 film *A Place in the Sun*, directed by George Stevens, who was an early member of the Actors Studio. The story is told primarily through reactions and the web of relationships between people rather than dialogue, description, declarations, or even action. Many of the camera set-ups include the full figures of more than one actor instead of individual close-ups.

The novel on which the film is based, Theodore Dreiser's *An American Tragedy*, tells a complex psychological story. The film adaptation relies on the technical ability of American actors to execute Russian techniques. Two of its stars became Strasberg-trained performers. Shelley Winters plays a trusting factory girl in love with a socially connected cad, played by Montgomery Clift. Winters, who would later become a serious devotee of Strasberg, has said that working with George Stevens on this film taught

---

*Unavailable to Strasberg's students.

her the principles of the Method even before she took her first class at the Actors Studio (26).

Winters's shy fragility is powerful and moving, especially the way she listens—still and silently wary throughout her increasing intimacy. Clift's obsessive attraction to another girl (Elizabeth Taylor) is established without his uttering a word, created entirely through his reactions to her wealth and beauty. His own lower social class is expressed by his wordless awkwardness in society. The scene where he wrestles with his task of drowning the factory girl (now pregnant) is dramatically heightened by the obstacle of her nervous chatter—motivated by her attempt to overcome the obstacle of his silent unease (her futile task being to make him love her again).

The Range and Limitations

Stanislavsky's techniques have also been influential in China and other parts of Asia. It was introduced in Communist China by the Russians as part of the Communist-approved art forms of Socialist Realism. A theater created by motivated actions was easier for mass audiences to appreciate than the traditional forms of Chinese theater, which played to the expensive, cultivated tastes of its elite public. A school of realistic plays was encouraged in China and Chinese actors learned Stanislavsky's techniques. Chinese playwrights studied Ibsen and Chekhov.

They continue to do so today, even though Russia and China stopped being comrades after a few decades. The authoritarian control of the arts in China means that certain topics are encouraged, certain others forbidden. Chekhov's ironic prophecies about a new wind coming are interpreted as meaning the eventual triumph of Socialism. But in 1996 a production of Ibsen's *Enemy of the People* took China by storm, demonstrating that Ibsen, after all these years, was still venerated as a great realist playwright and Stanislavsky-inspired actors were his dedicated interpreters.

Stanislavsky's revolution in the theater is permanent. No matter the country or culture, theater is an art of human relationships, and Stanislavsky's emphasis on compassion propels his system's survival past changing theatrical styles and national borders. Like Freud's interpretation of psychology, Stanislavsky's system offers genuine insight into the mechanism of behavior and feeling.

In America, Stanislavsky is the core of a serious actor's training, and most actors in this country are now trained to use an Americanized version of Stanislavsky's system of motivated actions. American universities and high school classes proudly teach aspects of the Method. Professional actors review Stanislavsky's technical vocabulary in studio classes. American students—and teachers—accept their duty to chase away hokey acting with zeal.

There is another mission, too, that actors inspired by Stanislavsky take on seriously: his appeal for artists who work onstage to love the theater in themselves, not themselves in the theater. Faith in the value of Stanislavsky's system, however, sometimes leads to disbelief in any other way to work.

Stanislavsky himself recognized no limitations to his system, although some limits were intended: no caricature, no talking to the audience, no exaggeration, no stylized speech or gestures. Stylization, though, is not necessarily a bad thing onstage. Some very good scripts are written in verse, involve caricature, or can only be performed while acknowledging the audience.

No art form, including acting, has any one way of working, any one true method. Scripts, audiences, interpretations, and the physical setup of performance vary and require different techniques. The painter working in watercolor applies the paint differently than when painting in oil. The technique of carving stone is very different from those of casting bronze or molding clay, yet any of these skills can create a sculpture.

There isn't any one way to interpret behavior, either. The unexamined prejudices of his society clouded even Freud's vision (his assumption that women were inevitably envious of men is particularly ludicrous). Stanislavsky experimented with stylization,* but accepted without too much questioning the assumption of his day that imitating reality was the highest calling of art. The commissars of Socialist Realism helped to shape this aesthetic by shooting dead those who disagreed.

Even without a gun to their heads, Russians are fond of realism. Gertrude Stein reported that in 1908 when Sergei Shchukin, a collector of Picasso's early romantic paintings, saw Picasso's newest work, *Les Demoiselles d'Avignon*, with its mutilated forms and unnatural perspectives, Shchukin wept at the loss for art. We recognize now that a stretched canvas covered with paint doesn't need to pretend to be a mirror to be art. The stage doesn't need to pretend to be a mirror, either. The theater can show us more than what we are; it can show us what we might be, or what we might avoid becoming.

This book teaches five approaches an actor can take while reading a script and developing ideas in rehearsal and performance. We've begun with Stanislavsky's system for organizing a text through analysis of its characters' tasks and obstacles. Why would we abandon such a good idea for anything else? Because, even though Stanislavsky tried to make his system universal, *it doesn't work with every script*. In its Russian developments or in its American variants, this approach is not always appropriate or the most useful way to work on texts by authors as diverse as Shakespeare, Sam Shepard, or Gertrude Stein.

The next part of the book examines Bertolt Brecht's idea of *episodes*; an approach, Brecht took pains to point out, that was bent on the *task* of sweeping Stanislavsky's compassion off the stage.

---

*Often disastrously, but persistently nonetheless.